INTRODUCTION

In 1943, a naval engineer named Richard T. James was stationed at Cramp Shipbuilding in Philadelphia and was tasked with designing the springs that would suspend delicate equipment on ships at sea, keeping them level in rough weather.

As the story goes, he was experimenting with tension springs and dropped one. Hypnotized as the spring fell to the ground, Richard had an idea—and the Slinky was born.

Of course, that's not the whole story. That's the story of how a helical spring became a toy, not how the Slinky, as a product, went on to sell over 300 million units before the year 2000.

It is, in short, a story of invention. But for every product with an origin story, there's an equally compelling tale that doesn't get told the story of how that product makes it to market.

In this book, we're not going to teach you how to invent the next iPhone (or Slinky).

Our mission is basic: we're going to teach you exactly how to take a new product to market.

Over the course of our careers, we've have launched countless new products and features for companies large and small, including Sony PlayStation, Google-backed Rocket Lawyer, and multiple early and mid-stage venture-backed startups. We've also worked for agencies that have consulted for hundreds of small businesses on go to market strategies.

This book teaches you how to apply the latest go to market tactics emerging from Silicon Valley, as well as the foundational strategic thinking from the

Kellogg School of Management.

We've broken the book into seven sections outlined below, each one covering a key pillar of any go to market strategy. Within each section, we break each component into its foundational elements, cover tactical execution, and pull in examples from our experience taking products to market.

1) Target audience

- Who are you trying to target?
- How do you identify and segment your target audience?
- How do you know if you're at product / market fit?

2) Value propositions

- Understanding core components of a value propositions: competitive advantage, positioning, unique selling proposition, and value
- Calculating product value with math
- Defining value propositions without math

3) Messaging

- 6-step progress for building your messaging framework
- Copywriting: how to do it + 4 tips to do it well

4) Go to market team

- Who's involved in bringing a product to market
- Choosing a team that suits your strategy Defining
- success metrics for your team

5) Demand generation

- 2 models for demand generation
- An example of a demand gen campaign 7
- common demand gen tactics

6) The marketing mix

- Calculating the marketing mix
- Building your marketing mix

7) Price

- The basics of value-based pricing 4
- common pricing tactics

By the end of this book, you'll understand exactly what you need to do to catapult yourself into the market, and make your product the next slinky.

PART 1:
TARGET AUDIENCE
Who you target

This part of the book is all about the WHO of your go to market strategy— how to select your audience, what to look for in a good target audience, and how to link your audience to your overarching go to market goals.

This chapter will cover:

- How to set the business goal that your target audience is going to help you achieve
- The role that supply and demand plays in target audience definition
- Common B2B / B2C segmentation tactics and strategies
- How to size your market
- Product / market fit

Before you select an audience, set a clear numeric goal

The big mistake managers make with going to market is jumping straight into the strategy without quantifying their desired outcome. The entire point of a strategy is that it's a means of achieving an objective. Without an objective, your go to market strategy is aimless.

Starting with a strategy is a recipe for disaster!

When I worked at Sony, I had identified the perfect target customer for a new product. It was a match-made-in-heaven. The needs of the customer aligned perfectly with what the product delivered. The strategy was perfect! But there was just one HUGE problem: the customer segment was just too darn small. Even if I sold the product to every single member of that segment, it would barely have made a financial dent. You must have a goal, such as a clear financial objective, before you have a strategy. In my case, my goal required an imperfect strategy (i.e. pursuing an imperfect target customer) because the goal was more important.

Here are some examples of clear, quantified goals that will help dictate your strategy:

- Generate $15M in one year
- Sell 100,000 units in 6 months
- Break even on development costs in 2 years
- Achieve 50% market share
- Grow brand awareness among segment B by 90%
- Grow purchase intent by 3% among segment A
- Grow Net Promoter Score by 30% among current customers in segment B
- Generate $1M in pipeline monthly recurring revenue (MRR)
- Generate 200 qualified sales leads per month

Example

One of the most effective ways of generating new leads is to be a guest speaker for an influential organization. I was reaching out to key organizations to schedule my CEO as a webinar speaker. This kind of marketing is very effective in building your company as an influential thought leader. The problem is that leads generated in this way can require a lot of nurturing before they are ready to buy. In the long-term, such as an approach makes sense. If your goal, however, is to generate x-number of qualified leads THIS QUARTER you shouldn't be wasting time on high-level, long-term content marketing. Your company could be burning through cash so quickly that it simply cannot afford to invest in long-term tactics. Instead, the smarter course of action is to focus on existing leads and get them to the point where they are ready to speak to sales reps. That requires building content that is a bit more product-centric and that covers very specific pain points rather than high-level aspirations.

Nothing will help you focus more than writing a clear numeric goal:

- You won't waste time on inconsequential tactics
- You won't choose a target segment that is too small or too large
- You will make smarter decisions on how to allocate your marketing budget
- You'll be able to hone in on the partners who will matter most
- You'll know what marketing budget to request

There's a reason you created this product so it shouldn't be that hard to write down an objective. If you're working at a tiny company, your goal might be to retire off the proceeds from this product. In that case, just put down $3M profit as the objective. That way you don't waste your time dealing with tiny markets and tiny marketing tactics.

If you work for a large company, your goal might be to generate $100M in revenue or to acquire 1M users without any clear financial target.

Just ask yourself one question:

> How will I know this product was a success or not?

Remember: If you're not the founder or CEO of the organization, make sure whatever goal you've set aligns to the goal of the business. In larger organizations, the goal of the new product will in part be defined by the organization's needs. The #1 way to do this is to ask what metrics are discussed in board meetings. What needles is the board of directors looking at, and how will your product help move them? That's the best thing you can do to guarantee business alignment.

Pick your target customer

I've worked with lots of companies that invested heavily in products only to see them fail miserably when they went to market. When it fails, people start playing the blame game:

- "Our PR agent wasn't very good!"
- "We didn't have the same features as our competitor"
- "Google Ads was a wasted investment"
- "On-boarding was too slow and error-prone"
- "Another product released at the same time!"

The list is endless. But in reality, these are symptoms of a failed strategy rather than causes of the failed launch. Strategic mistakes cascade through everything, and usually, a poor strategic decision results in tactics that don't work, no matter what your budget.

And the first strategic decision that usually gets made is choosing a target customer. If you choose the right customer, then you have a larger margin for error when it comes to executing your campaign. With that in mind, here's how you pick to right target customer.

Estimate supply and demand

You need to select a target customer or market that has enough demand to achieve your desired outcome. This is a surprisingly common mistake, so let's break it down a little into the common traps we see.

Scenario 1: No demand

First, you have a product where there truly is not enough demand to support the primary goal.

For example, let's say you're launching a new pet insurance product specifically for retired racing greyhounds. Great! That's a super niche audience, which means you can probably create a value proposition and messaging that's hyper-relevant to your target customers.

But let's say there are two million retired greyhounds out there, and you need 4 million to achieve profitability.

While your product might be great, there just isn't enough demand there to make the product work.

If you're in this bucket, then you need to pivot to serve a larger target audience.

Scenario 2: No demand…yet

This is all too common in the world of technology. An entrepreneur identifies a problem and thinks: "I can fix this!"

Currently, there's no market for their solution, but the potential market is huge, and they're going to crack it wide open.

This is called category creation and, if executed correctly, it can be extremely effective. Since you're all alone in the market, you tend to get first mover advantage and all the perks that come with that, including brand awareness, thought leadership, and zero competitors.

However, category creation is extremely difficult. There are years of zero or no profit and revenue, and you are usually required to spend huge sums of money on demand creation. That is, educating people about the problem you've identified, creating a demand for your solution. Only then can you start the process of demand generation and start to see returns on your marketing spend.

Most importantly, category creation is a long-haul play. And, if your product isn't sufficiently unique, you may find that your years of creating demand can be stolen by a newer, faster-moving competitor who swoops in once you've done the hard yards of category creation.

Scenario 3: A lot of demand…but a lot more supply

Another big mistake would be selling something that is oversupplied. If you market something that doesn't provide much superior value over similar products on the market, then you are doomed to failure.

This is why measuring supply is an important step in planning your go to market strategy.

Example

One of the biggest mistakes new Amazon sellers make is choosing overly niche products that generate miniscule revenue. A smarter approach would be to look at what is already selling well (using data from a resource such as Jungle Scout) and improve upon deficiencies that appear in product reviews.

Example

Publishers have the very difficult task of trying to estimate how well a new book, video game, movie, or similar product will perform in the market. This is particularly important because the bulk of the marketing budget is spent in one very narrow window of time. The way they overcome this challenge is by using "comps" or comparable products to see how well they performed historically. If you are selling a new product, look at how well similar products have done in the past to estimate demand.

There are various ways to estimate demand and supply:

- Look at how well comparable products are selling using tools such as Jungle Scout or your own historical records:

- Use Google keyword planner to see how many people are searching for a solution to the problem you sell:

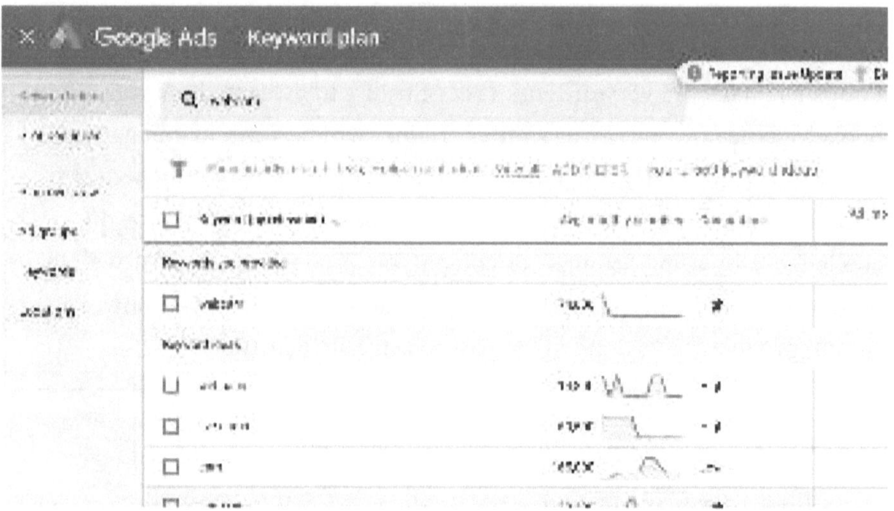

Google trends can help if you expect demand to grow or shrink. Some marketplaces such as Udemy will provide tools that give an estimate of both demand and supply:

Identify your target market

More goes into picking a market than just making sure you have enough supply.

Usually when marketers talk about target markets, what they're really thinking about are target customers. But this isn't quite accurate because markets include more than just customers. Imagine for a moment a physical marketplace—a place where people go to buy vegetables, clothing, and tools. There aren't just customers in that market; it is an entire ecosystem of buyers and sellers.

Focusing only on customers will get you into trouble. Airbnb, for example, cannot just focus on its target customers. It must also create value for the many people who rent out their homes—i.e., it must also focus on the sellers in the marketplace. Otherwise the entire two-sided market would fall apart, and their marketing strategy would be unsustainable.

A given target market actually consists of five components known as the 5Cs:

1. Customers: Who are you selling to? What problem do they have?

2. Company (in other words, your company): How do you solve your customers' problems? Where can you solve it better than the status quo / current solutions?

3. Collaborators (such as partners and influencers): Are you relying on partners, resellers, or platforms to help you get your product into the hands of your target customer?

4. Context (such as changing environment and regulations): Is there a compelling event that's driving a purchase now, or are there regulations you need to work around?

5. Competitors: Who else is in the market? Where do you win and where do they lose? How do people solve the problem right now?

A note on competitors

When we talk about competitors, we usually think about other providers of our product. For instance, if you're making a movie for Netflix, you might think of your competitors as all the other movies on Netflix. In reality though, your competitors are every single other way that your target audience can spend their leisure time. This might be playing video games, going to a movie, watching videos on YouTube, reading a book...It's endless. Another example is B2B software. While you might have competitors who people look at if they're considering your solution, your competitors are also how else they might solve the problem, which includes using software like Excel, getting consultants to do it, or just not solving it at all. When you're thinking of competitors you need to consider a much larger picture than just your category.

As you can see, choosing a target market is more involved than simply finding the ideal buyer. It requires studying the overall market and determining whether that is a space in which you want to participate. The customers in a particular market may be ideal, but if there are too many competitors active in the space, then it may not be viable. Alternatively, a particular market may seem unattractive because it has a lot of competitors, but if you happen to have collaborators with a lot of clout in that market, then it could be strategically viable.

As you design your go to market strategy, it's important to consider all of the 5Cs, even if only in passing.

Segmentation

As you build you go to market strategy, one of the first questions should be:

Who's going to buy this?

And that's a more complicated question than you might think.

There are dozens of different ways to define your target audience. Which strategy you choose will depend on your specific circumstances, but here are some tactics you can use to define your ideal client profile, or ICP:

- **Firmographically**: In business-to-business marketing, it is common to divide customers based on their industry, because in this case your 'customer' is actually an entire business.

- **Behaviourally**: That is, you divide customers based on certain behaviors such as how much money they spend or how much time they spend using your product. It is very important to focus on your most profitable segments.

- **Motivationally**: Overall, we would say that the best approach to segmentation is motivational. That is, you separate your customers based on their motivations for using your product.

- **Demographically**: Segmenting based on demographic information like gender and age.

These approaches to segmentation are not mutually exclusive. You can actually combine them or use different ones for different purposes—one for strategy and another for media buying, for example.

Most marketers rely on their intuition and arbitrary choices to segment the market. Often they don't realize they're doing this because they use quantitative data, which makes them feel as though they're being objective. Wrong. Quantitative data does not make your segmentation objective.

Usually, marketers segment based on industry, gender, usage behavior, or some combination of variables. The problem is that they've pre-determined which variables are important. How do you actually know that you should be slicing and dicing the market by industry or by gender? Why not by age? Or by income? Or by time spent using the product? Or by time of day using the product? How do you know which variables are most important to divide the market?

In marketing today, we're drowning in data. Because of this, you cannot look at the numbers and get an intuitive sense of what's happening. It's impossible. Humans are just too simple to see patterns in massive quantities of data. There is just too much complexity. That's where cluster analysis enters the picture.

Cluster analysis

Cluster analysis is one way to systematically approach segmentation and use data to drive your audience targeting, thus laying the foundation for everything else in your go to market plan.

Here's how it works.

First, you collect your raw data. For instance, you might send out a survey asking lots of questions about people's behaviors and motivations when it comes to the type of product you sell. You might ask about firmographic and / or demographic information, behavioural information, or motivational information (e.g. "what were you doing when you decided you wanted to buy a product in this category?")

Then, you then take the quantitative results and run a statistical process called a cluster analysis. This process automatically clusters all of the data you've collected into segments. Once you have the groups, you can see if those groups correlate to demographic or firmographic data. For example, group 1 might consist of people who spend a lot of time and money on their laptops. That group could also be predominantly male. While the group is determined by the continuous variables time and money, it correlates positively with the binary variable gender. A common go-to-market mistake is segmenting first with demographic or firmographic data when other data are often more relevant and easier to quantify. You're lucky if your segments align closely with demographic data because that makes targeting easier. Quite often, however, demographic data proves to be irrelevant. Usually customers segment based on needs that cross demographic and firmographic boundaries.

At the end of this process, you'll have a statistically relevant map of insights.

For example, say you're a software company who makes a data aggregation tool that syncs the sales and marketing tech stack and pulls out relevant data insights.

Once you complete your cluster analysis, you might find that midmarket companies (firmographically) start to look for a product in your category when they're trying to push for a Series B round of funding, and need to pass stringent due diligence (motivationally).

Used this way, cluster analysis can be a powerful way to segment and to choose your target customers.

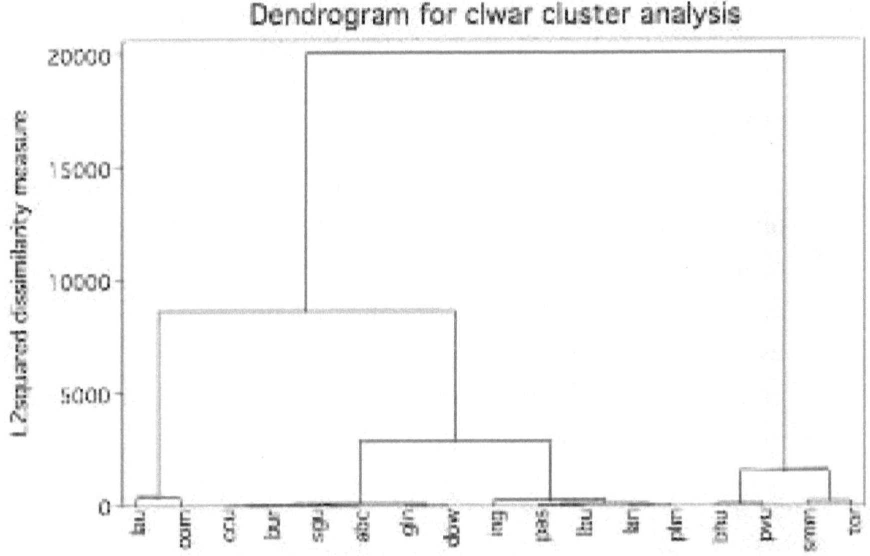

Reference: Phil Ender

This is a denogram—a visualization of what cluster analysis looks like. You can see here that are basically three different clusters of customers. Cluster analysis accounts for many different variables, so it's not easy to make simple statements such as "cluster 1 is rich people" and "cluster 2 is poor people." You need to look closer at the data to see how the clusters differ from one another on each variable.

The specifics of how to do a cluster analysis will vary depending on which program you are using (such as SPSS or STATA).

This work is absolutely critical to going to market. If you can understand the best people to buy your product, then you're going to be much more successful as you grow (and spend!) your way into the market.

How to do cluster analysis

Cluster analysis doesn't have to be some intimidating process that requires business intelligence tools and a Masters degree in statistics. Here's how you can cluster your data using Excel and your CRM / system of record.

Let's say you have data for 1,000 customers. This includes:

- Hard data from your accounting system or Salesforce or wherever that tells you how much revenue these customers generate for the company
- Product usage data via Pendo or a similar tool
- Purchase history for each individual customer
- Marketing data, like participation in various campaigns or referrals you've received from them

There are countless behavioral metrics you could be collecting. All this data exists in your database, but you might also have tons of data from surveys that tells you things like what motivates them to buy in your category or what keeps them up at night. How do you make sense of it all?

First, pull all the data out of your various systems and plonk it into a spreadsheet.

Assign the 1st column in your spreadsheet to your customers. Every column thereafter should represent the variables you've collected for each customer. For example, your 2nd column might be revenue, and your 3rd column might be time spent using your product per month.

Now you might start to see a problem here. Each variable is on a different scale. For instance, how are you supposed to compare revenue to time? If your revenue is measured in millions of dollars and your time is measured in dozens of hours, then the analysis is going to give undue weight towards the millions of dollars. That's why you need to standardize the data.

One way to do this is to convert each data point into a z-score. By converting each data point into a z-score, you can fairly compare the numbers. The way you get a z-score is by taking your number, subtracting the average, and then dividing by the standard deviation. You can learn more about this on Khan Academy.

So let's take the revenue column. You need to calculate the average revenue for all your customers, followed by the standard deviation. By doing so, you can then replace every dollar figure with the z-score. Next, do the same thing for the time column. Convert every time data point into a z-score.

Another problem you're going to run into is that some of your variables are going to be binary, such as sex, or non-continuous, such as state or country. One way to handle these variables is to simply omit them from the cluster analysis. Once you've produced the clusters, you can then determine if those clusters correlate with things like sex or country.

Once you have a spreadsheet with your customer data standardized, you can run cluster analysis using Stata, SPSS, R, Excel, or some other statistical program.

These programs will give you the option of producing a visual graphic called a dendrogram. Here you can see how your customer data tends to group into clusters.

The output of your cluster analysis might yield something like this. Suppose it generates four clusters; cluster 1 tends to be high in revenue but low on time; cluster 2 might be low in revenue and low on time; cluster 3 might be high in revenue and high on time; and cluster 4 might be low in revenue and high on time.

You can then run a correlation test between each cluster and the variables we couldn't test earlier, such as sex or country. You might find that cluster 1 tends to be skewed towards male.

So let's take cluster 1 as an example. This group is high in revenue generated, low on time spent using your product, and tends to be male. This could be the statistical foundation for a persona.

Using cluster analysis, you can pull together disparate data threads to tell a story that you can use in your marketing. And by identifying different variables that tend to correlate to profitable customers, you can spend your marketing dollars efficiently by appealing only to those who are going to actually make your organization money.

Look at your most profitable customers

One of the easiest ways to choose a target customer group is to identify who your top customers are. Take a look at your accounting software or CRM. List your clients in order from the most profitable to the least profitable. You may also need to make some assumptions depending on how sophisticated your record-keeping is. For example, you might need to use revenue as a proxy for profit.

Here is an actual example of a case I worked on. The company had a software system to collect information on transactions and customers. I exported this to Excel and then sorted the customers in order of the amount of sales they

generated.

If you have great many clients, I suggest that you split the information up into deciles. By this, I mean 10 gatherings. So the main decile will be the top 10% of clients as far as income or benefit and the last decile will be the base 10% of customers.

decile	total sales	% of sales	cumulative % of sales
10	504747.04	36.79341111	36.79341111
9	240036.77	17.4974212	54.29083231
8	165449.99	12.06043625	66.35126856
7	129976.97	9.474639201	75.82590776
6	105029.41	7.656092962	83.48200073
5	81980.83	5.975972402	89.45797313
4	58653.32	4.275519309	93.73349244
3	42394.6	3.090343921	96.82383636
2	30128.65	2.196220518	99.02005687
1	13443.26	0.979943125	100

Based on the measurable investigation I've done actually and the examination I've seen, your benefit is most likely being driven by a little gathering of clients. 80% of your benefit could be coming from pretty much 20% of your whole client base.

This is a similar case I portrayed before, just as opposed to introducing each and every client, I am introducing 10 bunches of clients. I took the all out number of clients and isolated that number by ten. That provided me with the size of every decile, and afterward I included the deals for every decile. I then partitioned that number by the absolute deals to the level of deals coming from that decile. To show up at the total level of deals, I just included the numbers from the third column.

So what does this information tell us? All things considered, it shows us that practically 37% of deals are coming from only the main decile! The main deciles represent half of the deals! This has gigantic key implications.

If over portion of your deals are coming from only 20% of your clients, then you might need to think about zeroing in on that gathering. The leftover gathering probably won't merit the work. If you can get more people who look like that top 20%, then you may grow a lot faster.

Now that you know where you income is coming from, you can do a bunch examination and see what joins these clients. You need to inquire: What issues would they say they were confronting when they came to you? What objections do they have?
Why do they continue to return to you? What convincing occasion drove their purchase?

Segmenting without historic data

The position a great deal of new businesses end up in is settling on a ton of choices around target market definition without a ton of existing information. At the point when this occurs (particularly assuming it's beginning phase) they return to offering to the crowd they know as opposed to the crowd that is the best fit for the item. On the other hand, they don't characterize the ICP precisely, and attempt to target everyone.

Neither is a decent arrangement. This is what you can do on the off chance that you don't have any data:

- Talk to prospects
- Identify where in the market there is evidence of under-served customers
- Try to answer these important questions and take action from there:
  - Where's your existing domain expertise?
  - Can you use that to accelerate sales in a specific domain?
  -

Is it valuable to tap a local network first?

Personas

Once you've distinguished your objective market (regardless of information) you really want to make a decison on personas. Personas are basically an individual you've made that addresses your objective purchaser. The thought is, you take your picked organization fragment, recognize who at that organization will be the person who purchases your item, and you make an individual to address them.

For instance, assuming you sell into moderate sized engineer-to-arrange organizations, and the individual at your objective association who's engaged with each arrangement is the Director of Mechanical Engineering, your pesona may be Mechanical Mike.

You'd layer on the demographic infortmation that you know about Mechanical Mike (male, white, 45-67 years old, married, etc...)

Then the motivational drivers.. (e.g. wants to do a great job, lots of pride in his work)

Then the stressors and agonies (needs more time, hard to adjust time at the workplace with time with his family, loads of involvement however not a major fanatic of progress, and so on...)

Finally, you'd bundle all of this data into a cheat card, so anybody in the association can comprehend your objective audience.

Persona's can be amazing assets, especially when they're founded on information. It's regularly simpler to make convincing efforts when you have an actual portrayal of individuals you're really offering to, rather than "engineering

organizations with more than $50 million in yearly

income". Nonetheless, be warned:

- Personas take an extremely long time to craft well. If you're strapped for resources, then there are usually other go to market priorities that should take precedence.
- The only thing worse than no persona is an inaccurate one. And marketing is often guilty of building personas that don't meaningfully help sales teams, or lead to creative that forges a meaningful connection with the audience.
- Because of the creative flair needed to craft a great, sticky persona, they often become traps for what marketing teams *suspect* or *wish* their audience was, rather than a useful reflection of what it actually is.

Market sizing

However you choose to portion your crowd, the following thing you really want to do is sort out the size of this main interest group to ensure that arriving at your objective's sufficiently large. This is called market sizing.

Basically, are there enough of your objective clients out there who can purchase your product?

Total Addressable Market (TAM)

One of the best-and most straightforward ways of showcasing size is taking a gander at the financial backer relations pages for public organizations in your industry. Regularly, public organizations will post financial backer introductions that accomplish crafted by estimating the business sectors for you. Frequently this is conveyed as far as a "Hat," or all out addressable market. For instance, on the off chance that you work in online business, take a gander at the data Amazon and Shopify distribute for their financial backers. Assuming you work in imaginative programming, shift focus over to Adobe.

Another method for measuring markets is to take a gander at information bases of lead records. In the event that you work sought after age, you might have bought admittance to a data set of organizations or leads. You can plug in the criteria you're looking for—such as revenue size and location—and the database will spit out how many companies fit that profile. Remember that the number you get will just address a small amount of the market (except if your data set has each organization in the business), so you should swell anything number you get. Ask whoever deals with the data set to appraise the amount of the market the data set covers. On the off chance that that gauge is 75%, you'll have to extrapolate by separating your numbers by 0.75.

A third way to deal with market measuring is to utilize the information organizations give you to free in their promoting stages. Whenever you pursue promoting with LinkedIn and Facebook, for instance, they will let you know the number of individuals or organizations fit the profile that you are searching for. You can utilize these numbers to appraise the number of clients are in your objective market. You can likewise do a similar title-put together measuring based with respect to government evaluation and work measurements information. Assuming you're focusing on a global market however, this cycle rapidly turns out to be incredibly tedious and difficult.

The fourth way to deal with market measuring is to see outsider exploration. A think-tank might have previously estimated the market. Simply look on Google and influence the exploration that is as of now been done.

The last way to deal with measuring markets is to do your own essential examination. You could go out and physically count individuals, items, or organizations, and afterward remove the example you gathered to the general populace. You could likewise do studies and extrapolate your information in the equivalent way.

Keep as a primary concern that there are a wide range of measurements that can be utilized to estimate markets. One is incomes or benefits inside a market. This data can emerge out of various sources including Statista, financial backer relations pages, or from statistical surveying organizations like Mintel. Another measurement could be the quantity of organizations or customers. Depending on your industry, other metrics may be even more important, such as order volume or pounds of material shipped.

Serviceable Attainable Market (SAM)

If your TAM is the absolute number of clients who might actually purchase your item, then your useful achievable market, or SAM, is every one of the clients who might actually purchase your item that you can really sell to.

For instance, assuming you make whistles, your TAM may be the worldwide whistle market. Yet, on the off chance that you can support clients in the US, then, at that point, your SAM would be the US whistle market.

SAM is normally geographic, however it doesn't need to be. You could sell plan programming, however just help English. In this way, your SAM would be the English-talking plan world.

Serviceable Obtainable Market (SOM)

Finally, SOM. Your Serviceable Obtainable Market is the segment of the market you can sensibly target and who you can hope to buy your item. Your division work from prior, or some other work you've used to distinguish your objective market ought to involve your SOM.

As a decent guideline, your SOM ought to be somewhere around two times as large as your income objective in a given time-frame. For example, on the off chance that you want to close
$10 million in income this year, the SOM you want to do that should be somewhere around $20 million. That is on the grounds that you'll begin to

see consistent losses once you arrive at half portion of the overall industry. As Geoffrey A. Moore makes sense of in Crossing the Chasm, when you hit the midpoint, catching the leftover half of a market turns out to be more difficulty than it's worth. All things being equal, you ought to change your go to advertise system, re-send off into another market, and do it tall over again with every one of the examples you've learned. This is known as the foothold technique.

Pivot! Pivot! The harsh reality of diminishing returns

All this work that you've now put into audience identification and segmentation comes with a vicious caveat—you're going to be doing it all over again, and soon. Why? Diminishing returns.

Diminishing returns are the point at which your publicizing dollars accomplish continuously more awful outcomes for the equivalent spend. Suppose you burn through $1 million structure mindfulness for your image. Your image mindfulness all in all, how comfortable individuals are with your image will without a doubt grow.

But it's truly challenging and costly to go from high brand attention to extremely high brand mindfulness, so you might need to distinguish where that articulation point is. Here is an example:

Month	1	2	3	4
Advertising spent	$0	$100,000	$100,000	$100,000
Brand awareness among target	0%	3%	5%	6%

You can see that assuming you don't spend anything on promoting, you will not have any brand mindfulness. But let's say that you start spending the same amount on advertising each month. Your image mindfulness leaps to 3% in month 2 and afterward to 5% in month 3. But in month 4, your brand awareness only increases from 5% to 6%. You contributed precisely the same sum, yet you're getting less return for that investment.

I remove a portion of that table and stuck it into Excel. I then inserted a graph to be able to see this visually. Do you see how the orange line gets less and less steep? That shows the consistent losses you face with this brand campaign.

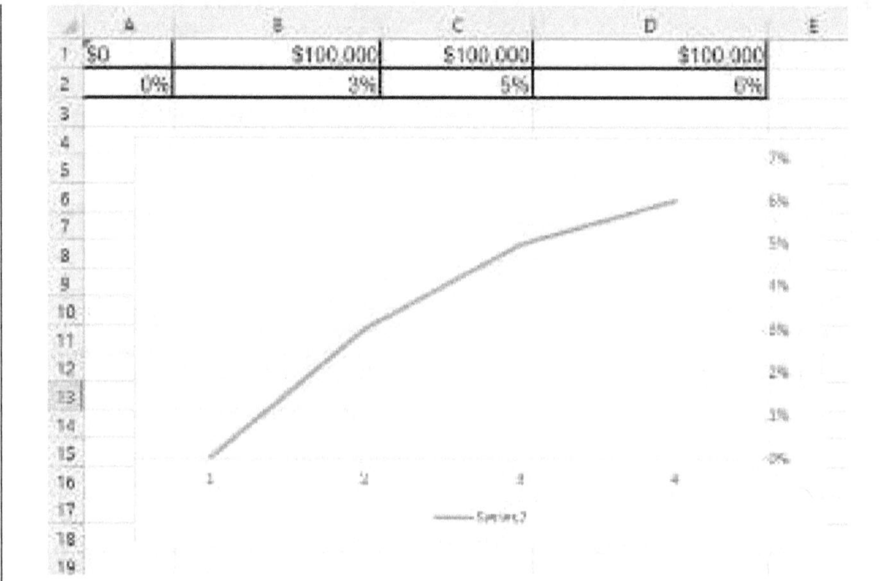

You need to decide as a team when it's time to pivot to maximize your returns.

Product lifecycle

As you can see, there are a ton of promoting choices to make. Also, one basic component is in the same place as you in the item lifecycle. Here you can see the average stages and deals bend that are utilized to portray the lifecycle.

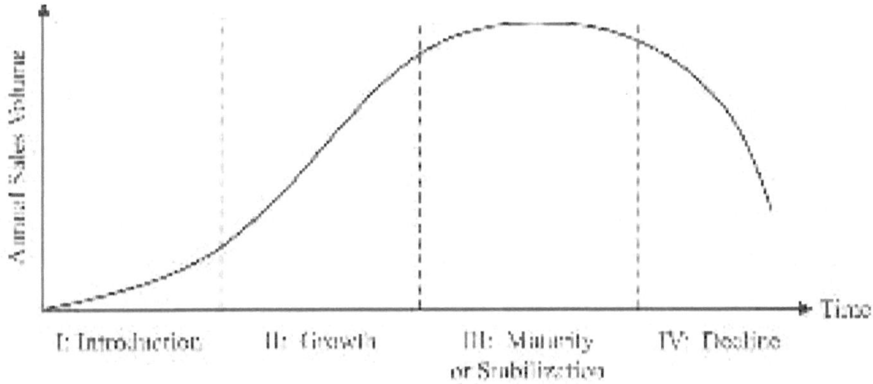

Reference: Wiley and Sons

A ton of thought administration in promoting comes from individuals who oversee items at the development stage. Frequently these items are purchaser bundled products from organizations like Procter and Gamble. At this stage, there's a solid accentuation on contest and cost-slicing to drive up overall revenues. There is likewise a weighty accentuation on monstrous brand advertising efforts as opposed to request age campaigns.

But for some go to showcase groups, the setting is totally unique. You may be working with items at the presentation and development stages. At these stages, you frequently don't have to zero in particularly on contenders. That is on the grounds that the market is developing and can uphold various competitors.

Moreover, brand mindfulness might be low to the point that clients simply don't know that you even have contenders. And on top of that, cost-cutting may also be less important. One reason for this is that growth will come from other sources, such as expanding revenue and a growing market. Your objective for this situation early adopters-are likewise frequently less cost delicate, so you can compensate for high costs with high prices.

In these stages, enormous brand showcasing is less important. You and your rivals likely haven't developed the economies of scale expected to put resources into TV crusades, for instance.

It's likewise important that in the beginning phases of an item's lifecycle, having a procedure at all can be troublesome. The item might change quickly to oblige anything that market signals you get. You have very little information on clients, and it's challenging to characterize what your objective market truly is. Also, your incentive may not be too not the same as your competitors.

I love system, however I should concede that in the beginning phases, experimentation can in some cases be a higher priority than vital planning.

Identifying and analyzing competitors

A vital element in choosing a market is getting the opposition. This is a two-venture process: (1) tracking down your in-market rivals, and (2) finding and getting your crowd's serious other options. Then, you're in a good position to develop compelling value propositions and messaging to drive your go to market strategy.

Step 1: Identify your in-market competition

This is presumably the most straightforward advance. The primary sort of contest is the one we're comfortable with: it's the organizations and arrangements you lose to after your ideal interest group has chosen to go through some cash on the problem.

So your initial step is to recognize who the contenders are inside your picked market classification. At times, this is simple. In any case, there are presumably contenders who you're not considering or who you haven't run into during your deals cycles.

Fortunately, there's bunches of ways of getting this information:

- Use tools like Crayon to track competitors
- Use tools like SpyFu, Google Keyword Planner, SEMRush, or Moz to identify competitors based on their online content and advertising strategies
- Look at category groupings on review sites like G2, Capterra, Yelp, or Google Reviews
- Hire people to research for you on Upwork or Fiverr
- Review other organization's web presences with tools like SimilarWeb
- Review your existing data and identify who you're losing deals to. Does anything unite the deals you lose to specific competitors (e.g. size, industry, etc.)?
- Complete win / loss analyses with your prospects. Who else did they look at during the sales cycle?

Once you have a rundown of contenders, you really want to begin investigating them.

First, take a gander at the upper hand every contender has. Upper hand fundamentally reduces to only two things: (1) economies of scale, and (2) customer captivity (e.g. churn rate).

- **Estimate economies of scale** by collecting data on your competitors, such as the number of employees, revenue, venture-capital funding, and social media followers. If you aggregate all of these, you can get a sense of their scale.

- **To assess customer captivity**, you want to look at things like subscription models, cancelation penalties, customization packages, and personalization options for their products. All these options make it more difficult for customers to leave. And from your perspective, that means your competitors are making it more difficult for you to capture their market share.

After looking at competitive advantage at the economic level, I then look at competitors in terms of marketing strategy. Here, you need to see things like what targets clients the contenders are pursuing and the way that they are conveying worth to these clients. Take a gander at their sites to see which verticals (ventures) they are focusing on. Take a gander at how they talk about their offer. You will get a feeling of the situating they are attempting to use to get in the market.

The third level I take a gander at is strategic. Take a gander at their estimating, bundling, item highlights, usefulness, and whatever else that could be significant, like notices. The drawback of this sort of examination is that it very well may be perpetual so you need to keep fixed on the top contenders you've identified.

To observe this sort of data, begin by scouring audit locales and talking about these issues with your possibilities. These discussions can be a goldmine for this sort of strategic data. By conversing with individuals who have experienced deals cycles with different organizations, you begin to get a sense for where those different organizations concentration, and what they pitch as their incentive. In the event that you're fortunate, you could even get a feeling of how your possibilities would answer your item offering, and you can begin to support your situation against those objections.

The most ideal way to assist with organizing this examination is a structure like the one underneath. This will provide you with a thought of market presence, nature of administration, and why individuals do or could do without them.

Competitor	Domain Authority (SEO Moz)	Site Traffic Rank (SimilarWeb)	Rating (G2)	Positioning From Reviews	Ease Of Use (G2)	Specific product weakness

| A | 47 | 100,000 | 4.0 | "intuitive" | 6.5 | x2 more expensive |
| B | 37 | 500,000 | 3.0 | "fast" "easy" | 10 | Doesn't integrate to |

						Salesforce
C	55	900,000	4.9		"affordable" 5.5	Low internal adoption

This initial step is generally direct; what's more difficult is outlining your serious alternatives.

Step 2: Identify your competitive alternatives

Competitive options are what your crowd would do in the event that your item didn't exist. I prefer to consider it such: If somebody was taking care of the issue you address, without getting you or any of the contenders you've distinguished, how might they do it?

For instance, suppose you make showcasing computerization programming. Your rivals may be HubSpot, Marketo, and Pardot. Your cutthroat options could be:

- Not doing email marketing
- Sending emails manually
- Only running email marketing through sales cadences via the sales team

Or say, for instance you make running shoes explicitly for running on treadmills. Your rivals may be Nike and New Balance. Your cutthroat choices could be:

- Swimming
- Other cardio gym activities (rowing machines, stair climbers, etc.)
- Barefoot running
- Other, less specialized footwear

Finally, suppose you will showcase with another computer game. Since you're principally offering fun in return for time, your serious choices are each and every other fun way somebody could invest energy. This includes:

- Other media (TV, Netflix, etc.)
- Hanging out with friends
- Hobbies or classes

When you ponder the client lifecycle, serious options will quite often start things out. Before Netflix went along, for instance, their clients were completely blissful leasing DVDs from a nearby store-until Netflix persuaded them that on-request streaming was what the future held. So the main thing you really want to do is persuade your ideal interest group that they need what you're selling by any stretch of the imagination. Then, when they're in-market, you want to persuade them that your item is the best.

Remember: You don't characterize the opposition or the market-your clients do. Which carries us to the issue of item/market fit.

Product / market fit

Marc Andreesen, the co-founder of Netscape and later, the co-founder of Andreessen Horowitz, defines product / market fit as *"being in a good market with a product that can satisfy that market."*

Essentially, item/market fit implies that an organization has accomplished three things:

1. It has found a business opportunity for its product
2. It has gotten that item under the control of (a portion) of its objective audience
3. s clients are for the most part content with the item and how it's tackling their problem

So, it's a blend of all that we've discussed so far.

For new companies, it is basic: put gruffly, assuming they neglect to track down item/market fit, they'll fall flat completely.

Even an astounding group, with an astonishing item has a little shot at progress on the off chance that it hasn't nailed its item/market fit to track down item/market fit. But an average team, with an average product, with *amazing* product / market fit will be incredibly successful.

Therefore, before you go to advertise, it's fundamental that you have item/market fit. Furthermore, that will appear to be unique relying upon your organization.

For new businesses, it implies you:

- Have secured some level of audience engagement
- Have a few customers under your belt
- Are generally getting positive feedback

You're possible dependent on originator selling and 1-2 incredible reps to get bargains across the line. Handling a deal is as yet nothing to joke about, and a refined, working deals cycle could not as yet be in place.

For bigger associations who are sending off new items, item/market fit will probably be an alternate monster. Better memorability, an all around demonstrated market, and a faithful crowd all make it a lot more straightforward to send off a new thing. Notwithstanding, those equivalent advantages imply that your outreach group, driven by quantities, will probably incline toward your current item line.

What's more, your situating, informing, interest group, deals materials, and contenders are reasonable all not the same as what your outreach group knows. It's important that you initially secure item/market fit-that is, selling a couple of arrangements, market-testing your situating, checking whether clients are cheerful before you truly go to advertise and include more resources.

Product / market fit vs go to market

So what's the contrast between tracking down item/market fit and going to market?

Scale.

Product/market fit is all observing your objective market with testing, repeating, and investigating novel thoughts until you recognize individuals who will cherish your item and are excited to give you cash for it.

Finding item/market fit is an intrinsically unscalable cycle, in light of the fact that the attention is on riffing on groundbreaking thoughts inconceivably rapidly until you strike gold. It's additionally less centered around building a repeatable interaction on the grounds that until you figure out your perfect balance, it's not worth the assets to ensure you can rehash it and again.

Go to advertise methodology, conversely, is about the capacity to execute and change over your item/market fit into repeatable, unsurprising revenue. Investing in individuals, cycles, and frameworks that mean you can dependably follow through on your income targets is the name of the game.

Product / market fit	Go to market strategy
Founder / VP Sales involved on every deal	Executive / leadership team is completely hands off on most sales
Sales process is loose	Sales process is buttoned down

Average contract value, conversion rates, and other core metrics are still in flux	Baseline metrics are well understood—ROI calculations product predictable results.
Focus is on MVP and iterative product / sales / marketing testing	Focus on process optimization to lower customer acquisition cost
Testing takes precedence over execution	Execution takes precedence over iteration
Inherently unscalable	Endlessly scalable
Marketing is focused on defining audiences, positioning, and messaging	Marketing is focused on generating demand within your target audience

Chapter summary questions

- Is your target audience large enough to support your business goals?
- Is there demand for your product beyond what the market is currently supplying, or are you creating demand for long term category domination?
- Have you identified your specific segments, including your TAM, SAM, and SOM?
- Do you know you competitors, competitive alternatives, and have you positioned your product to win against both?
- Do you have product / market fit?

PART 2:
VALUE PROPOSITIONS
Understanding your value

Now that you realize who you're focusing on, you really want to refine WHAT your novel offer for your go to showcase technique. Your incentive isn't an advertisement or a piece of showcasing guarantee. It's an interior apparatus to assist the whole with going to advertise group comprehend what you offer that might be of some value for your main interest group. All in all, your division, offer, and informing (which we'll address in the following area) structure the basic center your whole go to advertise approach.

In this section, we're going to:

- Define the key components that make up a value proposition
- Explain how to calculate the dollar value of your product
- Explore what to do if your value isn't attributable to a dollar figure

By the finish of this part, you'll comprehend what an incentive is, the place where it fits in your go to showcase methodology, and how to find one for your own product.

The value proposition

An offer is an essential part of your promoting procedure. It is every one of the advantages you are offering every one of the manners in which you make esteem archived and framed in a solitary spot. An interior apparatus will assist with zeroing in your advertising on the worth you bring to settle explicit agonies for your particular crowd.

A decent offer ought to be comprised of three unique parts: *upper hand*, *situating*, and USP. In any case, advertisers regularly utilize these terms conversely when truth be told they mean altogether different things. So we will jump into what every one is, and the way in which it connects with your worth proposition.

Obviously, it's within the realm of possibilities to go to showcase without each of the three parts. Be that as it may, the most grounded go to showcase procedure will be conveyed by associations who have various parts in place.

For instance, assuming you enjoy no serious upper hand over your next-best other option, yet you have extraordinary situating, you can effectively catch critical portion of the overall industry. Notwithstanding, you will be generally simple to uproot down the road.

That's the reason we prescribe while you're fabricating your go to advertise procedure and your incentive you attempt and anchor it to however many parts as would be prudent This would mean you foster extra item includes, ideal interest groups, or evaluating and bundling designs to check each incentive box.

Competitive advantage
Competitive benefit is a monetary term that implies a condition or situation that puts a particular organization is an unrivaled business position.

There are four normal kinds of cutthroat advantages:

1. *Economies of scale*: an organization can create a greater amount of their item at a lower cost since they're delivering a ton of it, which makes it hard for others to contend because of the minimal expense a particular organization can offer. Efficiently manufacturing suits versus tailor made suits are an illustration of this, where the efficiently manufactured suit can offer a greatly improved cost, and catch a greater amount of the market as a result of it, because of the reality they're making loads of suits without a moment's delay (and along these lines paying less to make each one).

2. *Customer imprisonment:* the expense and assets of changing to a contender are exceptionally high, so it's difficult for clients to switch. B2B membership programming (SaaS) regularly depend on this, since changing to another SaaS supplier will probably require execution, information, interaction, and individuals change-which are all exorbitant to the business and politically burdening inside for individuals involved.

3. *Enforced upper hands*: Government licenses can keep contenders from entering a market and deal an upper hand to the people who hold the licenses. Media communications, framework, travel, and energy organizations are frequently an illustration of this.

4. *Technology advantage*: When an organization has fostered a really imaginative item that is both patent secured and costly/difficult to duplicate. Drug organizations are a genuine illustration of this kind of upper hand when they foster another medication that can do what no other person can do.

A word of warning about technology advantage

It's not difficult to return to innovation advantage as your upper hand, particularly for tech organizations. The truth, in any case, is that most innovation organizations don't, as a matter of fact, have an innovation advantage. Indeed, they take care of an issue in a novel manner, yet all things considered, it's not adequately not the same as the following best choice to be a genuine moat.

There are special cases, obviously. For instance, for heritage arrangements, moving to the cloud is unquestionably asset serious, assuming it's conceivable by any stretch of the imagination. So cloud-first items have a huge canal. Another model is information. Gong.io, for example, is a business commitment and call recording answer for outreach groups. Their innovation records calls so agents and directors can tune in back on the call and mentor venders to improve.

However, that innovation is exceptionally simple to recreate. So Gong.io made an upper hand with information and AI. They examine every one of the calls of their clients, making a colossal information base of deals calls, and afterward utilized AI on those calls to fabricate an elite suggestion engine.

Their innovation advantage isn't their item's innovation, yet rather, a benefit in information and AI - the two of which are undeniably challenging to repeat quickly.

Unique Selling Proposition (USP)

Your extraordinary selling recommendation is the single explanation that separates you from both the opposition in your class and from the following best other option. It ought to be a blend of a basic list of capabilities, the advantage that the customer

gets, and how that connects with the aggravation you address for.

Obviously, this is frequently basically the same as your situating as we'll find in a moment. They distinction is that your USP is exceptionally explicit. It's a solitary component/include put that puts you aside from everybody else.

For instance, assuming you were selling a gaming framework, one interesting offer may be selective privileges to a particular game that is just accessible on your system.

By focusing on a hyper-explicit list of capabilities/benefit, you make it exceptionally obvious to your potential clients why they would get you over another person. It's anything you can highlight and say:

This is the means by which we're unique in
relation to everybody else!

Defensible USP

One test that new companies specifically have is finding a solid USP. What we mean is that your USP should be inarguably interesting to you, unmistakably upheld by information and social/outsider proof.

For instance, a ton of organizations need to make client care their USP, in light of the fact that they're incredible at it, and their clients love it. But is that defensible? No. Except if you've won an honor, or been perceived by experts like Forrester or Gartner, or you'be the most elevated positioned organization on something like G2, it's not something you can solidly say "we are awesome." Plus, you'll need to look long and hard before you observe an organization who says "we have horrendous client service."

Rather, your USP ought to preferably be something your rivals say "no, we don't don't do/have that."

Otherwise, it's extremely easy to counter in a head to head and it makes it hard for the customer to understand why they should buy you instead of someone else.

Positioning

Finally, situating. *Situating is the decision about which part of your item you will zero in on to increase the value of your interest group.* At the end of the day, situating is tied in with having a special interest in say:

This is what our identity is and the way in which we help. In the event that you don't need this, then our item isn't for you.

Obviously, this is staggeringly unnerving. You're not kidding "our item isn't really for this sort of client," and we address this in more detail in the following area on messaging.

For now, however, there are a couple of things about situating that merit calling out now:

1. Positioning is basic. You really want to effectively choose what makes you unique.

2. Positioning frequently feels like it ought to be self-evident, however it seldom is. Keep in mind: what gets you invigorated is likely not exactly the same thing that gets your clients excited.

3. Positioning is as much about getting out whatever you're not as what you are. It's enticing to be something for everybody, except that seldom works.

4. Every item is situated. Possibly it's finished by you telling the world what you are and what you do, or its finished by the market, letting you know what your identity is and what you do.

Once you've distinguished these three center parts, you can begin to continue on to the last advance of illustrating an offer: really working out the worth to clients of your solution.

Value: how customers benefit

Value is the dollar sum that clients get back when they purchase your item. A basic model may be your item costs $100, and it saves your client $500. Your worth is $400.

Value is normally extremely dry and numerical, and is something that you really calculate.[1]

For instance, saving individuals large number of dollars on ointment costs each month, or decreasing their request handling time by 1 minute.

Even in the event that your item doesn't truly set aside your clients cash it might in any case set aside them hypothetical cash that is, the cash that they would somehow need to spend in the event that they didn't take on your solution.

Calculating product value

Calculating worth can be intricate, yet the hypothesis is simple.

First, distinguish the expense of sitting idle - proceeding to live with the pain.

Then, compute the expense + advantage of taking care of the issue another way. This may be a competitor.

Finally, check your own item out. What's the expense of your item, and what kind of return would your clients be able to hope to get?

Let's say your product is an energy efficient lightbulb for factories. Compared to a regular light bulb (e.g. the cost of doing nothing), it might save your customer $10,000 per year in expenses. Your customer is also looking at other energy-efficient lightbulb providers (your competitors).

Maybe your best rival can save them $8,000 each year in costs. Assuming that is the situation, your worth is $2,000 far beyond the following best alternative.

This table lays each of the expense investment funds out:

Cost savings	You	Competition	Difference
Electricity	$10,000	$8,000	$2,000
Labor	$5,000	$6,000	-$1,000
Oil	$1,000	$1,000	$0
TOTAL	$16,000	$15,000	$1,000

So, you can fundamentally bring down their power costs, their work costs, and their oil costs, contrasted with an ordinary light. Contrasted with sitting idle, the worth you add is $16,000. Since you truly do have some contest, the worth you offer contrasted with your next-best option is $1,000.

When it comes to incentives, you really want to take a gander at your worth contrasted with the following best other option, since that is the way the client will check it out. You want to say "we offer $XXXX of extra worth contrasted with the following best answer for your problem."

Let's gander at another model. This is a genuine incentive I dealt with for a product item. As the table shows, that worth came from three fundamental sources: investment funds through stock, investment funds through computerization, and reserve funds through returns.

Savings from decreased inventory	$375,000
Savings from automation	$59,904
Savings from fewer returns	$1,350,000
Product price	$22,360

As you can see, the main investment funds was through returns. In fact, it was so much larger than the other two that it really helped us focus our USP and positioning on the problem that we solved really, really well. Since we contributed such a lot of significant worth through lessening returns, that turned into our center situation in the market.

In these two models, the worth comes straightforwardly from cost savings.

But recall, there are a couple ways that an organization can offer value - cost saving is in no way, shape or form the just one.

For instance, your incentive could incorporate steady benefits as opposed to simply diminished costs. A steady benefit is the worth that a client acquires when an item adds to their income. (We utilize the term 'steady' here in light of the fact that for each dollar your item adds to income, it just adds a part to benefits so the worth here is the gradual benefit added).

Why bother calculating value?

Many advertisers depend on informing to drive esteem, zeroing in on what clients need to hear as opposed to zeroing in on where the item adds value.

But as the models above represent, a digit of math can assist you with measuring the worth that your item makes in your objective market. What's more, whenever you've done that, you'll make some simpler memories pitching to your objective audience.

Let's say you're selling programming that computerizes when lights turn on and off in large business structures. How would you offer this to possibilities? "Mechanize your lighting!" "Save time with programmed lights!" "The best lighting software!"

There are various methodologies you could take with these features. Furthermore, odds are most would come up short. That is on the grounds that you haven't really distinguished the worth that you are creating.

You want to break it down.

How does your product truly help the business? How can it influence the benefit condition: Profit = (Price - Cost) * Quantity?

There are a couple of opportunities for how your product could drive value:

- Because the lights are automatic, that might mean that customers don't need to hire staff to go around turning lights on and off. That could cut costs.
- The lighting might foster a special mood in the building, or a more pleasant customer experience. This could help boost revenues.
- The lights might spend more time turned off, reducing energy costs.

When advertisers do situating, they frequently surmise about which advantage is generally significant and assemble crusades around that. But a more sophisticated approach is to actually calculate how much value is created from each possible benefit, and run the one that offers the most value.

So, of the three advantages, suppose that lower energy cost is the one with the most worth. Without a doubt, the reserve funds for a singular structure may be negligible, yet when these expenses are scaled across at least 10 structures, the energy investment funds are significant. Presently we're focusing on the primary advantage of the value

recommendation: bringing down the client's energy costs. En route, we've better characterized the objective client: organizations with at least 10 enormous stores or structures. These possibilities have significant energy costs, so cutting costs turns out to be more important.

With this data, an organization can put the most important advantage - for this situation, lower electric bills - at the core of its situating, making a lot more grounded case for clients as it goes to market.

What to do if you can't calculate value

Math is without a doubt your companion with regards to incentives. But there are a raft of products that provide significant value that can't be calculated easily. Either the worth isn't financial in any way, or the worth is theoretical it's not something you can undoubtedly connect a dollar figure to. This is especially normal for B2C companies.

For instance, envision you were showcasing Coca-Cola. In fact, for the client the dollar esteem is the calories and satisfaction they're getting at a low cost. Obviously, that is not the way in which Coca-Cola markets itself. All things considered, the worth it gives its clients is cool. It creates and markets an image of what a Coke-drinker is, then sells the drink as the path to achieving the image they've created.

So, in the event that a dollar esteem isn't a piece of your incentive, you really want to zero in on convincing use-cases for your interest group. What is the number 1 most important value that your product brings to the table? And why do they specifically want to access that value that your product brings?

Let's return to our Coca-Cola model. In the event that the worth they give is a cool picture, they could fit that worth to explicit crowds. For instance, assuming they were focusing on grandparents, they could zero in on how Coca-Cola can assist them with interfacing with their grandchildren, in light of the fact that it's a cool beverage. Then again, if Coca-Cola was focusing on youngsters, they could zero in on how Coke can make you famous at school, since that likely cool means to teenagers.

Your value proposition does not need to be unique

Here's a last note on incentives: they don't constantly should be unique.

Marketers invest a great deal of energy attempting to sort out their USP. Furthermore, this is surely a beneficial activity yet you don't constantly have to accentuate how remarkable your item is.

For instance, you may be selling something a non-vital buy, like plastic screws. Your purchaser likely doesn't mind what makes your item extraordinary they simply need something solid at a sensible cost. For this situation, underlining uniqueness is a misuse of time.

Or, suppose you're working in a shiny new, creative market. Your clients could have no information on your rivals. For a situation like this, it's useless to underline how you're unique in relation to your rivals. All things being equal, simply center around imparting how you make value.

Chapter summary questions

- Does your product create enough value for the customer to be worth buying?

- Have you identified your competitive advantage, positioning, and unique selling proposition?
- Have you calculated the value you add to your customer, and linked it to a specific benefit / feature?
- Have you tied your value calculation to your USP, positioning, and competitive advantage to build a complete and robust value proposition?
- Can the value you create be measured in dollars and cents, or are you bringing a more nebulous concept of value to your customers?
- Have you identified the part of your product that brings the most value?

PART 3:
MESSAGING
What to say and how to say it

Messaging is the manner by which you enlighten the world regarding your item. It responds to the inquiry: WHY would it be advisable for me to purchase this? It overcomes any barrier between: (1) situating, where you characterize what you sell, who you offer it to, and the worth they get; and (2) request age or promoting, where you enlighten the world concerning your product.

If you have a firmly characterized crowd and a reasonable incentive, you're in a decent spot to foster incredible informing. Extraordinary messaging:

- Tells your target audience what you do and why they should buy you
- Uses the language your target audience uses
- Surfaces the problem your audience has, and drives action to solve it
- Communicates the value you provide

You need to construct an informing structure that gives you both the adaptability to play in different channels and across crusades, yet at the same time remains laser-zeroed in on tackling the issue you've characterized. Your informing structure ought to likewise attempt to emphatically construct your image equity.

One inquiry I get a great deal is: "What's the point of messing with all of this? Our outreach group knows what to say and who to say it, too!"

It's a decent inquiry. Building an informing system is tedious and can feel somewhat repetitive. However, actually without a framework,

your informing will float off kilter as you run various missions, produce various bits of content, and recruit new agents for your becoming go to showcase group. To stay with your item and your moving in lock-venture towards your goal, you really want to keep everybody on message, constantly. And a messaging framework is the best tool to do that.

The cycle I frame for building an informing system in this section depends on the Pragmatic Marketing Framework and the situating book Obviously Awesome by April Dunford. I've utilized it to construct informing structures for complex B2B items, and it does something amazing for keeping your informing focused.

In what the future held, stroll through the 6 stages you really want to go through to assemble an incredible informing framework.

Once we have those 6 stages under control, the remainder of the section will zero in on copywriting. This is the opposite side of the informing coin: If your informing structure assists you with working out what to say, copywriting is tied in with sorting out some way to say it. The copywriting part of the section offers a couple of fundamental dependable guidelines that will assist you with discussing successfully with your objective audience.

Building your marketing framework

Building an informing structure can appear to be a mammoth undertaking. Be that as it may, it can really be separated into 6 reasonable steps:

1. Find the elements your crowd cares about
2. Find the upside of your chose features
3. Link your benefits to value
4. Group the advantages you offer by themes
5. Map values to personas and assemble use cases
6. Build the framework

In this part, we bring a profound plunge into every one of these means, taking a gander at why they matter and how to execute them effectively.

1. Find the features your audience cares about

Your item has many highlights. You really want to show them hard and fast, then select the ones your crowd really focuses about.

On example, say you sell TVs. Your item has loads of highlights, including:

- A black stand
- A power cord
- Plug and play software
- A remote
- 4K resolution

Of these elements, obviously the 4K goal is the element that the interest group will think often about. Having a remote presumably won't persuade anybody to buy.

At the finish of this progression, you ought to have a refined highlights rundown of things your item does that your crowd really thinks often about. There are a couple of ways of getting this information:

- Talk to your existing customers (if any) about what features they love about your product or competing products.
- Review old support logs or call transcripts. Are there consistent requests to address a problem that your new product solves?
- Talk to your product owners. Why did they recommend building a feature in the first place?

2. Find the advantages of your selected features

Now that you have your highlights, you want to characterize their benefits. A benefit is the reason you incorporated a particular element. It's the positive result that your element creates.

If we return to our TV model, the upside of 4K goal is perfectly clear picture quality. Benefits ought to be somewhat simple to think of, since you probably fabricated the item with a particular goal in mind for a particular reason.

3. Link your advantages to value

People don't buy elements or advantages, they purchase the worth, or benefit, that they get from your item. Esteem is the "so what" of your item highlights and benefits, and on the off chance that you can plainly convey the worth of your item and do it in the language of your ideal interest group you're armies in front of generally go to advertise teams.

Most informing stops at benefits. That is on the grounds that connecting your highlights to esteem and advantages is very difficult. It requires profound client information, as well as sympathy to get what they're battling with.

What makes this doubly trying for go to showcase groups is that they realize the item so well-and when we know an item, we're for the most part truly adept at depicting what it is and what it does, yet not very great at portraying why somebody ought to mind. It's so instilled in us that it's difficult to express. We lose the woodland through the trees.

The outcome is that most groups go to advertise with elements and benefits, and cause the customer to make the actual worth. But it doesn't need to be this way. By driving yourself to plainly depict among benefits and worth, you can work on your item to get to the center explanation that somebody would get it. So how would you make this significant qualification among benefits and worth?

The most effective way to move from benefits to benefits is to take a gander at each benefit and inquire, "So what? For what reason does our crowd care about this?"

Let's return to our TV model. The element is 4K goal. The benefit is perfectly clear goal. What of it? For what reason would it be advisable for me to think often about the goal? All things considered, the advantage is that you'll feel shipped to anything you're seeing on the screen.

For certain items especially intensely commoditized items with heaps of rivalry you could possibly depend on your crowd to change over the benefit into an advantage themselves. That is the reason we frequently see advertisements for buyer tech items like earphones, cameras, and TVs that basically ramble highlights like they're clear benefits. For example, a TV promotion may very well say "4K goal in your family room," or a camera advertisement may very well say "the new iPhone has a 12MP camera!" These items don't need to make sense of the "so what" since buyers have sufficient setting that they definitely know.

However, depending on this is a risky game:
- It makes it harder to differentiate your product as competitors copy your feature and advantages, so it can leave you vulnerable to alternative providers
- Your audience might only translate your features and advantages in one specific way, whereas you might be able to think of more (and more compelling) value

One of the most ideal ways to get from benefits to esteem is to converse with your interest group. Tune in for what they whine about, could do without, or battle with. What do they wish was different in their expert or individual lives, and where do those needs cover with your answer? Such conversations can give you the understanding you really want to get to your item's "so what's."

At the finish of this stage, you ought to have a table that looks like this:

Feature	Advantages	Value ("so what?")
What does the product do?	What's the advantage for our target audience?	So what? Why does our audience care?

4. Group the benefits you offer by theme

As you work out your advantages, You'll probably see a few subjects arise. That is, numerous benefits and elements ordinarily lead to comparative advantages, or advantages integrate conveniently into a package.

Therefore, the subsequent stage is centered around classifying endlessly heaps of values into a couple of significant pails. As you go to showcase, you'll see which fragments of your crowd answer best to which topic, and can tailor your campaigns

accordingly.

5. Map values to personas and build use cases

You want to plan all that you've done to your objective personas (on the off chance that you didn't assemble target personas, essentially map them to the important individuals in your purchasing panel - the gathering of titles typically associated with your deals).

Take your subjects and see where they fit most actually. Normally, this matching will change as you go to showcase and realize what's working and what isn't, however it's great to have a beginning point.

It's likewise important to make use cases that guide to your personas. Assuming you know the worth you convey, how is the utilization instance of that esteem different for various personas?

Take our TV once more. The worth is that it transports you to anything you're seeing on the screen. That is an extraordinary beginning, however it's pretty generic.

To make it really convincing, you can fit it to personas with use cases for every one. For example, assuming that a section you're focusing on is avid supporters, the utilization case may be "transport yourself to the large game".

It's basically a similar worth, it's only reevaluated to suit the audience.

6. Build the framework

Your last advance is to placed all of this in a system, which you can use to comprehend what you say, why you say it, and to whom.

It's likewise useful at this stage to make short rundowns of your item. I like a 1-sentence synopsis, a 2-sentence rundown, and a 5-sentence summary.

These outlines are shockingly valuable, both as an activity to consolidate basically everything you've done down into something tiny, yet in addition as a resource for have close by. They prove to be useful all of the time: reps can draw on them when they're practicing their elevator pitch; you can drop them into bios of executives if you're featured in the news; and they can even act as a functional anchor to keep discussions about your messaging tight.

At the end, you'll have a structure that looks somewhat like this:

The audience Who are you targeting? Who loves your product?			
1-sentence summary The value of the product in 1 sentence.			
2-sentence summary The value of the product in 2-3 sentences.			
5-sentence summary A short paragraph explaining the product and how it helps your target audience solve their specific problems.			
	Values theme 1	**Values theme 2**	**Values theme 3**
Persona 1	Use case	Use case	Use case
	Benefit	Benefit	Benefit
	Advantages	Advantages	Advantages
	Relevant features	Relevant features	Relevant features
Persona 2	Use case	Use case	Use case
	Benefit	Benefit	Benefit
	Advantages	Advantages	Advantages
	Relevant features	Relevant features	Relevant features
Persona 3	Use case	Use case	Use case
	Benefit	Benefit	Benefit

	Advantages	Advantages	Advantages
	Relevant features	Relevant features	Relevant features

You may be believing that this is a great deal of work to wind up where you as of now are. But building your messaging framework—and putting it down on paper in this concrete way—is critical. It not just makes your informing much more straightforward for other inside groups to consume and comprehend; it additionally compels you to stand up to your pondering why a particular advantage is significant, and everything highlight set best says to the account of that benefit.

It's likewise important that in spite of the fact that you'll assemble your system from highlights down to utilize cases, your structure ought to work the other way. So when you set your structure up as a regular occurrence, you ought to zero in on the granular, explicit worth that you bring to your clients first, prior to jumping into how you make it happen (benefits) and what you really sell (features).

Once this last advance is finished, you're prepared to handle copywriting. Your informing structure has effectively set out what to say. Presently, now is the right time to sort out some way to say it. That is the place where copywriting comes in.

Copywriting

It's difficult to discuss informing without looking at copywriting. Copywriting is the means by which your informing advances out into the world.

Of the multitude of parts of go to showcase system, copywriting is likely the most misjudged. Frequently, when individuals hear copywriting, they envision Don Draper devising trademarks like "It's toasted!" on the spot for clients. They picture inventive organizations concocting things like "Got Milk?" or "Wazzzzup" or "On the grounds that you're worth it."

In all actuality however, copywriting is tied in with conveying the worth of your item, to your crowd, as obviously as conceivable in a way that urges action.

It may be really imaginative and innovative...but it likewise could not. Regularly, viable copywriting is truly straightforward.

Here are five basic guidelines to assist you as you with speaking with your objective audience.

1. Speak directly to the buyer—and do it conversationally

Some of the most grounded words in copywriting are words like "you" and "your." You need to talk straightforwardly to the purchaser as you would in a one-on-one discussion, and you need to do it in language that they use everyday.

To accomplish this, attempt to follow these four guidelines:

1. Use a conversational tone. This implies keeping away from scholastic, proficient discourse that is excessively formal or syntactically right. For instance, stating, "for example, may be syntactically right when you're going to show a few models, yet in all actuality, a great many people would basically say "like." Generally, the best copywriting has a more casual, conversational ring to it.

2. Write in the subsequent individual, like you are talking

straightforwardly to the purchaser. For instance, "Computerize your bookkeeping," is better than "Mechanization for bookkeeping." It's more private, it talks all the more straightforwardly to the crowd, and it's additionally really convincing and order. You're let your crowd know what they, explicitly, will actually want to do once they purchase your wonderful product.

3. Write in the current state. This takes the theoretical future advantage and causes it to appear to be more unmistakable. For instance, "Get a sweetheart" is better than "You will get a sweetheart" or "You will have a sweetheart." Note here the utilization of the basic state of mind writing such that orders or requests.

4. Write in the dynamic tense. In fact, this implies that the subject plays out the activity of the action word in a sentence, as opposed to the subject being followed up on by the action word. For those of you who aren't dynamic individuals from the language police, this essentially implies that your composing will have significantly more effect. For instance, "Get 10% off" has much more power than "10% off will be had by you."

One of the most straightforward basic guidelines is this: keep away from the words "be" and "by" in your copywriting. It won't work constantly, yet it'll help a lot.

2. Witty, brief headlines usually aren't effective—keep it straightforward

advertisements that attempt to be astute are seldom successful. More often than not, it's smarter to go with a more straightforward feature that imparts how your item creates

value.

There are countless aimless features out there that attempt to be brief or astute. You know the ones-perhaps there's a period after every single word, or some theoretical joke posted on a bulletin. But here's the thing that you've probably noticed: these ads don't usually drive you toward a desired action. Best case scenario, they give you a laugh and cause you to have a warm and fluffy outlook on the brand behind them.

As a rule, it's smarter to simply get to the center of how your item makes esteem. You can do this by zeroing in on the results that the client needs. For instance, "Twofold your pay in one year," or "Save $10,000 in energy costs." These features convey the worth accomplished from whatever you're selling.

When it comes to composing features, something else we prompt is to write in the sentence case. That is, capitalizing only the first word of the headline and proper nouns. This allows you to compose longer, more clear features. And it'll help you avoid short, witty, and confusing ones.

3. Cheesy, salesy writing works

At the strategic level, I think most about us have lost the specialty of salesy copywriting. Throughout recent many years, it appears advertisers have fallen into the propensity for creating copywriting that understands well and is even a piece formal, to the detriment of charismatic skill. But the truth is, cheesy salesy writing works better.

John Caples demonstrates the viability of this style in his books Making Ads Pay and Tested Advertising Methods. The advanced interest age master Howard Sewell likewise exhibits this in his article "However Wait, There's More! Why Cheesy Copy Still Works."

So what sort of composing is effective?

- Phrases like "But wait, there's more!"
- Use of the ellipsis instead of proper sentences so that the reader is encouraged to keep reading…
- Short, punchy sentences.
- Incorporation of enthusiasm (many writers seem to lack enthusiasm in

their writing).

- Promising quick results.
- Phrases like "announcing," "introducing," "new," and "free."
- Making specific promises such as "You will make $100,000."

Remember: these expressions will be different relying upon what you're selling. Being salesy possibly works if your salesy offer is something that your crowd wants.

4. Stay on brand

Staying on brand implies utilizing language that is predictable with the brand-and this is perhaps the main thought in powerful copywriting.

Many organizations will have a brand guide. But if not, you may need to make one from scratch in order to keep your copywriting on brand and on message. The brand guide ought to frame what sort of character your image has, and it might even meticulously describe the particular kind of copywriting that you ought to be attempting to execute.

Here's a model where brand consistence is significant. This is an advertisement for Metromile. Notice the interesting verse first and foremost and the utilization of "Ta-da." This is an exceptionally relaxed and amicable brand. It seems as if Metromile has any desire to be your friend.

Reference: u/cawatoons on Reddit

If you were composing messages for this brand, you'd need to be predictable and utilize this amiable language. This is significant in light of the fact that consistency will assist with building a solid brand position in your client's brains. Irregularity, then again, weakens your image positioning.

Brand guides can get significantly more explicit than this. They could even incorporate a few complete expressions that you can pull. Each component could have key list items that have previously been checked by marketing specialists or leaders in your company.

5. Be persuasive

We can't exaggerate how significant this is. Recollect our definition prior: copywriting is conveying the worth of your item, to your crowd, as plainly as conceivable in a way that constrains action.

That last piece-propels activity is vital, yet it frequently gets neglected. Copywriting is generally about evolving conduct. That could be convincing possibilities to purchase an item, utilize a component, click a button, put stock in your organization, or to take some kind of action.

The idea chief on influence is the teacher Robert Cialdini, who is popular for his book Influence. These are his vital drivers of persuasion:

- **Scarcity**. People are motivated to take action if they believe something is scarce. For example, using the phrase "Three days left!" persuades people to act because whatever you're offering is only available for three days. If it were available all the time, there's no sense of urgency. People prioritize things that are time-sensitive. People could do without missing out.
- **Consensus**. People are motivated to do things if they believe other people are doing that same thing. Social proof is an incredibly strong persuasive tactic. A good example of this is "90% of people prefer." If 90% of people prefer this option, then the user will likely choose that action. Some people are non-conformists, of course, but the vast majority of people rely on consensus or social proof to make

decisions. This is particularly true in situations where the user isn't informed enough to make a decision on his or her own.

- **Authority**. People are persuaded if someone in a position of authority tells them to do something. Using phrases such as "Dr. Joe Stephens" or "the expert in this field" will persuade people.

- **Reciprocity** is also an important consideration. As humans, we have a compulsion to reciprocate when we are given something. Giving people something for free could motivate people to take action in return.

- **Consistency**. People want to be consistent. If they told you something in the past, they want their future actions to be consistent with what they said. You could remind people of what they did in the past by using phrases such as "Since you enjoyed…" This may prompt people to buy something or take an action consistent with past actions.

- **Lastly, people are persuaded by things they like**. Using cheesy phrases such as "You are awesome!" can give your product more persuasive power. User experiences with this type of language can be particularly pleasant. Flattery is a powerful tool for building your brand personality and giving your brand product persuasive power.

Copywriting Example

This example of Udemy's messaging helps illustrate some of the major copywriting rules of thumb that we've covered in this chapter section.

Let's beginning with influence. Udemy is truly accentuating a urge to get going by utilizing shortage. "1 day left!" "End of the week Sale," "Put your fantasies first today." They're not drawing on other influence strategies like agreement or authority, yet there are traces of enjoying here. "Put your fantasies first," for instance. Individuals will more often dislike it when discussions revolve around them. And the *your* is also important here. Personalization itself is a helpful device for influence. This informing additionally features a significant point: few out of every odd message you compose requirements to utilize each strategy without a moment's delay yet great informing will typically use somewhere around one.

The copywriting here is likewise immediate. It tells the purchaser precisely what they ought to do (put their fantasies first by exploiting Udemy's deal) and the way in which they'll benefit, and it utilizes every one of the right syntactic shows to drive that activity: it's written in the subsequent individual and it utilizes the present and dynamic tenses. It's additionally genuinely conversational. None of the language is intricate or scholarly. It reflects how Udemy's clients really speak.

And at long last, the feature is clear and it keeps away from the impulse to be clever or astute. Notice how they've separated the message into two sections ("Weekend Sale" and "Put your fantasies first today and learn for just $28.99). The initial segment is short, sweet, and forthright. The second is longer and more included and it's composed as a full sentence. Utilizing a full

sentence here lets them write a longer, clearer, and ultimately more informative message.

Chapter summary questions

- Have you defined your feature set, linked your features to advantages, connected those advantages to your value and benefits, and grouped similar value / benefits together?

- Have you built a messaging framework to be used across your go to market team?
- Have you zeroed in on your copywriting and messaging to make sure the go to market team is telling the right story in the right way?

PART 4:
GO TO MARKET TEAM
Who needs to get involved?

Going to advertise is a group activity. There could in fact be a go to showcase "proprietor" (and in more modest associations, this could even be the CEO). At the end of the day, it's a cooperative effort.

Generally, go to showcase groups are comprised of each and every individual who contacts the client all through the client lifecycle: deals, promoting, and client achievement or support.

This section plunges into the subtleties of the HOW of going to advertise with a unique accentuation in the go to advertise group and their different jobs and obligations. The section is partitioned into three segments, each zeroing in on a specific fragment of the go to advertise group. We center around making sense of the job of:

1. Marketing, item advertising, and request gen
2. Sales in high-and low-ACV settings
3. Customer success

Marketing

Marketing frequently drives the go to showcase methodology since they have such a lot of impact from the beginning (as you could have seen, promoting covers the majority of the phases of go to advertise technique that we've covered up until this point). Showcasing groups are likewise all around situated to lead the go to advertise technique since they associate item, deals, and client success.

When it comes to go to showcase, promoting's job is partitioned into two huge branches:

Product marketing

Product advertising's job is to do all that we've illustrated up until this point: characterize the crowd, recognize the market, characterize the incentive, make the informing, and framework the channel mix.

Oftentimes, item advertising is vigorously engaged with both inner and client confronting content, including:

- Research papers, blog posts, and webinars
- Battlecards, sales wikis, and persona documents
- Case studies

Demand generation

The job of interest age is to additionally characterize the channel blend, execute the real advertising efforts, and emphasize and test to drive down the expense of gaining customers.

Each of these capacities can likewise cover extra specialized topics, including:

- Field marketing
- Brand marketing
- Content marketing
- Digital marketing

In more modest associations, these capacities are regularly totally run by a couple of individuals, with item promoting taking on satisfied and brand, and request gen taking on computerized and field marketing.

Sales

Sales is liable for a certain something: shutting business. This capacity is basic to such an extent that most associations take drastic actions to keep their outreach groups roused and laser-zeroed in on that and just that.

How you approach deals with your go to advertise group relies upon your normal agreement esteem (ACV). Why? Since deals implies headcount-the most costly piece of any go to showcase strategy.

That implies that you should sell something adequately significant to legitimize a salesman and their compensation (in addition to make the commission worth their time).

For example, say you're selling cell cases online for $3.99 each. That worth isn't sufficiently high to legitimize an outreach group. Then again, in the event that you're selling development gear for $10 million, it's most certainly worth the sales rep's salary.

Generally speaking, B2B deals merits having that high-contact, 1:1 deals experience in light of the fact that the ACV will in general be higher. Then again, B2C floats towards low-contact, conditional, hands-off sales.

High ACV sales (B2B)

High-ACV outreach groups going to advertise are organized like this:

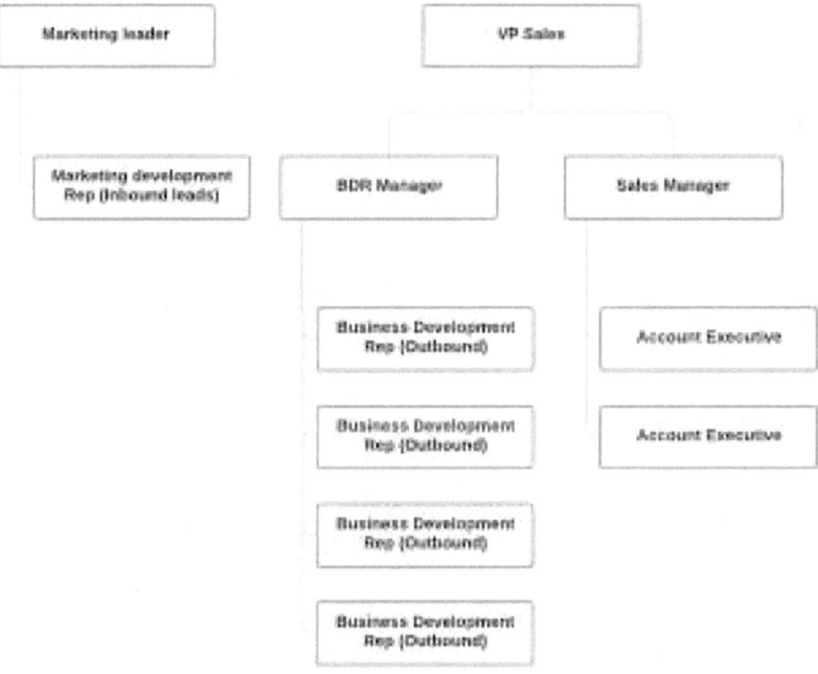

- *Marketing development reps* are responsible for responding to inbound leads. These teams increasingly report into marketing rather than Sales.

- *Business development reps* are responsible for outbound prospecting, and booking meetings for account executives to close business.

- *Account executives* are responsible for handling the meetings that inbound and outbound reps book and taking customers from an initial meeting to a closed deal. Account executives might be field reps, on the road and visiting customers in person, or part of an inside sales teams.

When you're fabricating your go to showcase technique, you really want to painstakingly consider the number of reps you will require and in what the future held explicit business objectives. This goes for huge and little associations, on the grounds that at a little one or a startup, you're choosing the number of bodies to employ, and at large ones you're choosing the number of bodies to commit to the item. In the two cases, you're submitting huge assets, and that implies that you really want to consider cautiously about how you will accomplish a positive ROI.

Sales operations

There is one more basic deals work that you really want to go to showcase deals tasks. For any business, the way to fruitful got to showcase execution is twofold:

1. Finding a valuable open door for development in your association's information (or the market assuming you're a beginning up)
2. Understanding and adjusting your strategies/technique on the fly in light of early pointers you find in deals information as it rolls in

For example, say you're offering tractors to moderate sized assembling firms. Your business cycles may be a year long. But you don't want to find out a year down the line to find out your positioning is all wrong, or your messaging isn't resonating. You should follow information en route to improve your transformation rate at each progression of the deals cycle.

And, on the grounds that outreach groups are the front line of client collaborations, they're the ones that really assemble the information that different divisions and use it to make decisions.

Which implies you really want a reasonable deals process before you go to advertise so you can follow execution after some time and check whether your go to showcase drive is on target to accomplish your in general goal.

It's regularly worth recruiting (or getting a consultant) to assist you with setting up your go to advertise deals interaction and ensure you're catching the information you really want as possibilities go through the purchasing process.

Low-ACV sales (B2C)

Sales teams usually play a much smaller role in B2C organizations (or B2B organization selling to small businesses) because the average contract value is low. Instead, the final point-to-point sale is executed through a different, transactional mechanism. This can be through a channel / distribution partner (e.g. if your product is stocked in a store or sold on Amazon), through an ecommerce store that you control, or in your own store.

Customer success

The last significant part of the go to advertise group is client achievement. This is the group that guides clients from when they sign an agreement, through execution, and on to proceeding with progress. For programming as an assistance (SaaS) organizations who depend on clients reestablishing to accomplish benefit, client achievement is basic since they're answerable for keeping the clients that deals closes.

Notwithstanding their execution and backing liabilities, client achievement is progressively liable for recharges, upsells, and strategically pitches, basically on the grounds that upsells and strategically pitches are incredible for a business. Upsells and cross-sells:

- Ingrain your company into the lives of your customers, decreasing customer churn
- Increase the customer value as they purchase more product

In particular however, you've proactively invested a major lump of energy and assets to obtain them. The more worth you can extricate from them, the better your profit from investment.

And in the event that you remember client accomplishment for the go to advertise group, you can decisively get clients who will develop into high-esteem accounts over the long haul. Client achievement can drive benefit because:

1. Word of mouth possibly occurs assuming you have cheerful clients. And since word of mouth has proven again and again to be the most cost- effective marketing channel, ignoring it is literally leaving money on the table. Verbal exchange is particularly significant on the off chance that you're a little or

   obscure brand/startup, when each client is basic to your general achievement.

2. Client obtaining costs are too high to not hold. For membership, freemium, and "attempt before you purchase" items specifically, maintenance is basic to the financial aspects of your association. You really want to keep your beat rate low. But even for companies selling one-off products, it's far less expensive to keep a customer than acquire a new one.

3. Upsell/strategically pitches depend on cheerful clients. You won't buy a greater amount of something assuming the association you bought from sucks. To drive high-edge strategically pitch and upsells (high edge since you've proactively paid to obtain the client), you really want to have cheerful clients, and that implies putting fundamentally in help and client success.

Churn and retention

One of the center measurements for client achievement is beat, particularly for membership benefits that depend on client maintenance to grow.

Churn rate can be determined two different ways: income agitate is the percent of your income you've kept throughout a particular time period.

For instance, assuming you had $100,000 of month to month repeating income (MRR) in January and $80,000 of MRR in February, your stir rate would be:

$$Churn = \frac{(\$100,000 - \$80,000)}{\$100,000} = 20\%$$

Basically, 20% of your month to month repeating income from last month isn't
going to repeat this month since it left. You can do a similar estimation on a yearly reason for yearly repeating income (ARR).

The second Along these linesrt of stir is client beat, or logo agitate. This is a similar estimation, yet rather than taking the income esteem, you count the quantity of clients. So, assuming we return to our model from prior, that $100,000 in income may be 100 clients, and 10 clients left. Your logo beat would be:

$$Logo\ churn = \frac{(100 - 90)}{100} = 10\%$$

Churn is vital to know in light of the fact that each dollar you produce is a dollar of new business you want to proceed to find. Assuming that your stir gets excessively high, it turns out to be unquestionably challenging to grow.

You can likewise utilize agitate to assist with your division. Here is an example:

Segment	A	B
Churn rate (unsubscribers per month)	3%	6%

Here you can see that fragment B has a higher beat rate, with 6% of endorsers leaving the assistance every month. It may be the case that section B is simply not an ideal objective client gathering, or it may be the case that you really want to make a few changes to make them cheerful and keep them want more. Information can't actually stop for a minute to do. It should be deciphered with regards to your general organization vision to conclude which move to make. The arrangement here isn't clear in any way. All we know is that bunch B is bound to withdraw than is bunch A.

Customer lifetime value (LTV)

Closely connected with stir is client lifetime esteem, or LTV. *Client lifetime esteem is a proportion of how important a client is to your organization.* It's very muddled to work out, so I will begin with a rearranged approach.

Year	1	2	3	4
Profit	$1	$2	$2	$0

This table shows the benefit coming from a specific client in every year since he turned into a client. You can see that he quit turning into a client in year 4- consequently, the $0 in benefit so the lifetime of the client is 3 years. The lifetime worth can be determined by including the benefit for those three years: $1 + $2 + $2 = $5.

The client lifetime esteem is along these lines $5.

This is a straightforward recipe. A more complex strategy addresses the universe of money. This more intricate equation represents agitate rates, the expense of client procurement, and something many refer to as the rebate rate. Allow me to make sense of. In years 2 and 3, you can see that benefit was $2. But since of the time-worth of cash, cash today is worth more than cash tomorrow, so that

$2 in year 2 is really worth more than $2 in year 3. That is on the grounds that $2 in year 2 might have been contributed and appreciated for a whole year. But there are other factors here besides the time of value. There's likewise chance and vulnerability related with future benefits that don't matter to the present.

Lifetime esteem is simpler to work out assuming your organization depends vigorously on client relationship the executives programming or CRM. If your company doesn't use CRM, then you may need to estimate lifetime value based on

testing clients through market research.

What you might find is that a portion of your clients are really losing you cash. You ought to make an honest effort as an advertiser to stay away from these sorts of clients. In the event that they leave you, don't send them limits or offers to return. Attempt to zero in your interchanges on the most beneficial segments.

Closely associated with lifetime esteem are these other metrics:

- **ARPU**: Average revenue per user. Be careful with this metric because averages can be deceiving. Often the bulk of your revenue comes from a tiny group of people. In that case, an average would be a misleading figure.

- **ARPPU**: Average revenue per paying user. In some markets such as free-to-play gaming, the bulk of people may pay nothing. That's why the average revenue per paying user may be more meaningful.

The explanation we're discussing these measurements here is that they're staggeringly significant for client achievement. In any event, client achievement (as a component of the go to advertise group) has the obligation of decreasing or taking out stir. Progressively, they're likewise answerable for developing records, expanding ARPU, ARPPU, and LTV. Assuming you're depending intensely on development to arrive at your objectives, you really want to watch these measurements like a hawk.

Assembling your team

For a B2B organization to convey a firm go to showcase methodology, they need to have advertising, deals, and client progress in place.

Marketing is expected to distinguish the market opportunity that the go to showcase group will take advantage of. Fundamentally, they answer the inquiry: where are we going to showcase and with what? Generally, the errand of addressing this question is possessed result advertising. But marketing is also needed to inform and convince people to buy (in a low-ACV environment) or talk to sales (in a high-ACV environment). This assignment is possessed by request generation.

Sales is expected to transform leads into shut business. Basically, deals is answerable for really taking the item or administration and getting it under the control of customers.

And client achievement is expected to enchant clients so they stay close by for quite a while. Client achievement likewise needs to keep clients blissful with the goal that they can be upsold business as usual or strategically pitched extra items while additionally telling the world how incredible you are.

Once these three sections are set up, you have what Jim Collins, in his book Good to Great, has called the flywheel. Basically, promoting gains clients, deals closes them, and client achievement delights them...which thusly drives securing, deals, and enjoyment, onwards and onwards as you assume control over your picked marketplace.

Chapter summary questions

- Have you assembled your complete go to market team, including marketing, sales, and customer success?
- Are clear roles, expectations, and SLAs defined across the go to market team?
- Have you calculated LTV and churn and linked both figures back to

your overall business goal so you know the benchmark values for both?

PART 5:
DEMAND GENERATION
How to build demand for your product

Demand age is tied in with getting the ideal individuals to set up their hands and say "I might want to converse with a sales rep about your item/administration." Essentially, it's the WHERE of go to market.

Demand age is particularly basic in the B2B world, where (a) each arrangement is worth more (and you can in this way spend significantly more cash obtaining every client) and (b) purchasing is a tedious, long, and cooperative cycle including loads of moving parts and various individuals. This part will:

- Cover the demand generation process, theory, and stages
- Walk through an example demand generation campaign
- Identify the most common demand gen tactics
- Demonstrate a full demand gen channel mix

The demand-generation process

The interest age process is moving from somebody who doesn't have the foggiest idea who you are to the fact of the matter they're prepared to assess your answer. Assuming you consider this adroitly, it looks like a funnel:

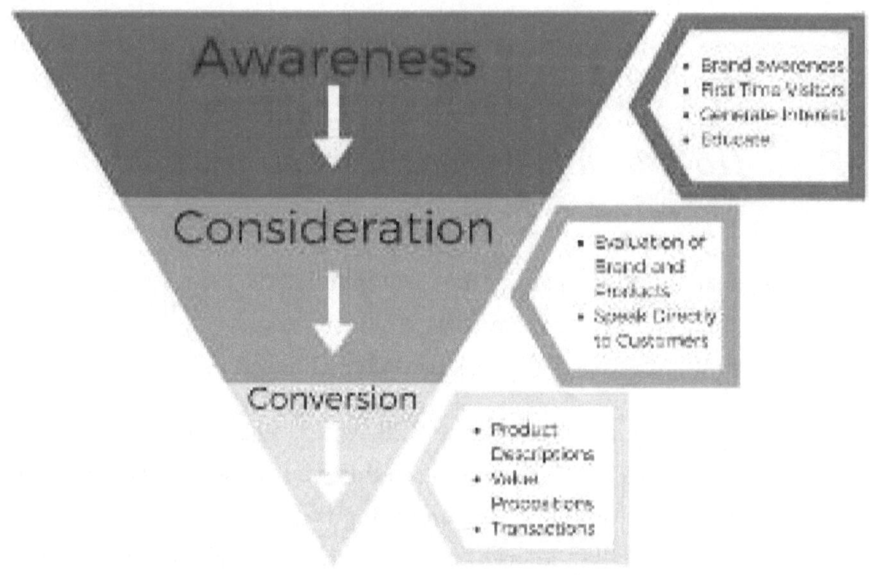

Reference: SEMrush

Awareness

Awareness is the stage when clients don't have the foggiest idea what your identity is for sure you do. They should be taught and made mindful of your image. The objective here is to be useful. Assist them with learning things that are fascinating. Assist them with tackling an issue they have, regardless of whether they utilize your device to get it done. Normal tactics

and channels here incorporate contributing to a blog and SEO, and brand mindfulness crusades where the center is essentially to get your name before target clients. Out of home missions, TV advertisements, force to be reckoned with promoting, and impression-based online entertainment advertisements can all play in this arena.

Consideration

Consideration is when they're looking at different vendors, and are considering you as a potential solution. They know who you are, they know the problem they need to solve, and they're considering if you can do it. The goal here will depend a lot on your sales process. For some businesses, this is when you put them in touch with a sales team. For other organizations, this is when you continue to promote content, but content that requires a bigger time commitment from your prospects (e.g. webinars, white papers, recorded demos).

Evaluation

Evaluation/transformation is when forthcoming clients are taking a gander at your particular arrangement, and are assessing you in much more detail. This is the point at which you're best situated to discuss yourself. In the event that it's a conditional business, this is the point at which the buy occurs. Key resources incorporate item and estimating pages, free preliminaries, and internet business buying. For bigger, more mind boggling items, possibilities at this stage are ordinarily "gave off" and enter the deals cycle.

Alternative model

Another structure for displaying the client choice excursion is introduced underneath from McKinsey and Co:

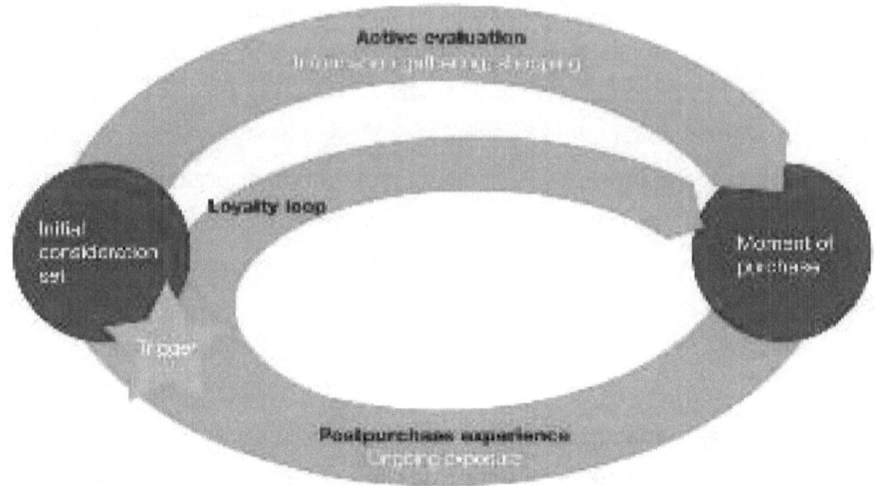

Here you can see the significance of trigger occasions that start the purchasing system. This could incorporate occasions like changing bookkeeping programming, extending to another store, getting a separation, or moving.

Demand generation ≠ lead generation

One of the most concerning issues with request age is that everyone discusses how they need more leads…

… however nobody knows what a "lead" really is. I could do without to utilize the word 'leads' since there are an excessive number of boundlessly various sorts. Here is a demonstrated interaction with different sorts of leads:

Reference: Saasmql.com

Awareness

- MCL = marketing captured lead. These may be cold leads acquired from a purchased list or compiled by your team.
- MEL = marketing engaged lead. These are leads that have some soft engagement with you such as filling out a form to acquire a white paper or webinar, or visiting a booth at a trade show.

Consideration

- MQL = marketing qualified lead. These are usually leads that have responded to a "high-bar" offer such as a demo, consultation, or price quote. Sometimes MQLs are just leads that accumulated enough lead scoring points that they are handed to Sales, even if they haven't actually requested an offer that would in and of itself qualify them to address Sales.

Evaluation

- SAL = sales accepted lead. These are leads that have been handed to Sales that are accepted rather than rejected and are being followed-up by Sales.
- SQL = sales qualified lead. These are leads that engage with Sales.
- SQO = sales qualified opportunity. These are leads that are candidates for buying your products within a reasonable time frame and have potential revenue (pipeline) associated with them.

The non-linear demand process

Demand age has gotten a ton of flack lately, essentially on the grounds that the above model seldom reflects how an individual finds an item and chooses to purchase from them. For example, say you're selling B2B software. Someone probably won't know about your item, however see your posting on an audit site. They'd hop quickly to consideration.

Likewise, aim channels like Google Ads imply that leads can enter your pipe at any stage. While this has generally been the situation (all things considered, a salesperson can continuously call somebody who says "really indeed, I'm assessing arrangements at the present time!") it currently happens much on a more regular basis. The pipe is as yet beneficial, and on the off chance that you're following productively, you can utilize it to see where you want to refine your go to showcase strategy.

Remember: your channel doesn't address the excursion each lead takes to turn into a customer.

Demand gen campaign example

Let's incorporated what we recently covered. This is the way an interest gen mission could unfold.

Step 1: Buy a list of prospects.

Once you know what sort of clients you need, you can proceed to purchase a rundown of 10,000-20,000 individuals who fit your objective. There are heaps of rundown dealers and providers out there, yet attempt to observe somebody who can you the most particular rundown for your market. Likewise consider testing a couple of test records from various providers. I've had a ton of trouble with providers giving extremely low quality records and being exceptionally late with conveyances. So the prior you can get on top of this, the better.

It's worth thinking about how you want to filter your list as well. For B2C products, demographics are almost always the starting point (e.g. men, 25-34 years old who make over $75,000 a year). For B2B companies, the starting point is usually firmographics followed by job title.

But those are just to begin. There are boundless ways of cutting up your possibilities to get the client you want.

For B2C, you could fragment by area, past buys, interests, propensities, brands they follow, or social stage activity.

For B2B, you could section by organization development, office development, number of areas, what innovation they at present use, group size, or organization age. The fact is, the better you can tune your channels while you're buying contacts to match your ideal client, the good you're going to be.

Note: It's ideal to compose a white paper that adjusts well to the issue your item settles or the yearning your item helps make a reality.

Step 2: Write a white paper.

This ought to be something instructive that tends to an aggravation or goal of your objective clients, for instance, "10 Tips for Generating $5M Selling Clothing Online." You can make the white paper in a Google Slide and basically trade as a PDF. You could likewise make it in a Google Doc, InDesign, or quite a few programs.

Step 3: Advertise the white paper on Facebook and LinkedIn.

Prospects ought to need to enter, at any rate, their email address to gain admittance to the white paper. The explanation we are publicizing the white paper is on the grounds that it's a decent top-of-channel offer. Other offers such as "request a demo" or "get a consultation" are bottom-of-funnel offers that don't perform well when promoted to cold leads.

Remember: you are publicizing the white paper, not your organization and not your item. A significant idea popular age is that you need to advance the actual deal (and the advantages of the proposition) as opposed to your organization or item. For this situation, the proposition is the white paper.

Step 4: Promote the white paper through content syndication.

Promote your white paper all over utilizing content partnership. You could, for instance, pay the firm PureB2B for each white paper download. Not exclusively will they elevate your paper to your objective clients, yet they'll likewise recognize the subset of individuals who are prepared to buy.

Step 5: Nurture the people who download the white paper.

Add individuals who download your white paper into an email arrangement in a program like Outreach. For example:

- Email 1: "I saw you downloaded the whitepaper "Title Name," so I thought you might like this video on "topic name."
- Email 2: "Here are a few tips to achieve x…"
- Email 3: "Here's a video of someone who achieved what you want to achieve."
- Email 4:" I can teach you how to achieve x. Are you interested in learning more?"
- Email 5: "I can show you the fastest, simplest way to make this pain go away. Book a demo with me, and I'll show you how."

At the finish of this mission, you ought to have produced some showcasing qualified drives that deals can change over into potential open doors, and afterward into won deals.

The key is to assess the complete expense for the number and worth of chances made, then, at that point, income created, then choose two things:

1. Was the ROI on this crusade positive? Essentially, did you get more cash out than you put in?
2. Was this the best utilization of promoting dollars? This question frequently goes un-asked, however each and every dollar spent on showcasing has an open door cost of a mission you didn't run.

Consequently, regardless of whether a mission has a positive ROI, there could have been a superior allotment of resources.

7 Common demand gen tactics

Now that we have a thought of the nuts and bolts of interest gen, we should take a gander at the most widely recognized strategies you're similar to use as you send off your new item. It's relatively easy even for a small team to use all these tactics, and as we'll see when we turn our attention to the marketing mix, using multiple tactics is usually the most effective campaign strategy.

1. Acquire leads / customers through Google and Bing ads

Google and Bing PRomotions are especially viable at gaining leads rapidly in light of the fact that they're expectation centered channels. That is, you can offer on watchwords that individuals are looking for when they have the purpose to buy. The weakness is that, over the long haul, pay-per-click advertisements aren't generally so practical as different strategies like substance promoting. That is on the grounds that the result from pay-per-click advertisements is by and large direct, as demonstrated by the expression "pay per click." conversely, happy showcasing, **PR**, and marking create economies of scale over time.

Another vital benefit of search promotions is that they can target individuals at the lower part of the channel i.e., the people who have a high buy plan and will converse with a salesman. You do this by focusing on explicit catchphrases attached to your answer, such as:

- How do I integrate X with Y?
- Best software for X?
- Buy X

What this implies is that web search tool publicizing can rapidly move the needle on pipeline and deals in manners that other advertising, (for example, white

papers) cannot.

One of the primary keys to progress is having committed PPC presentation pages. You by and large would rather not immediate PPC traffic to your landing page. You need to make a page that forces individuals to finish up a structure (or now and again, to purchase your item). For instance, you could request that individuals "Book a demo" and give a ton of social verification with regards to why you are awesome, like appraisals from outsiders and testimonials.

2. Acquire leads through Facebook and LinkedIn ads

Facebook and LinkedIn offer amazingly point by point segment and firmographic focusing on information, so you can serve centered promotions to your particular purchaser personas. The test however is that Facebook and LinkedIn promotions don't reflect aim. You can focus on the specific individuals who normally purchase your item, yet not individuals who are hoping to purchase your item right now.

So leads generated from Facebook and LinkedIn should generally be connected to a lead nurturing program, such as a series of emails you send out via a sales engagement (Outreach, Salesloft) or an email automation system (HubSpot, Pardot).

Intent vs behaviour example

I worked at a B2B SaaS startup called Upchain. We used both Facebook and Google Ads to drive leads. We first started with Google, bidding on keywords relevant to our product with the call to action "book demo." It was going great, so we decided to roll out Facebook ads, too. We directed them to the same high-converting landing page. But our conversion rate plummeted! Why?

Because our Facebook audience wasn't ready for a demo. They had no intent to purchase now, but they were the right people to purchase eventually. So we changed our approach. We switched our CTA on Facebook to a whitepaper all about how to build and scale the manufacturing tech stack (a problem we solved really effectively). Then, we nurtured these leads over time with content-focused email marketing. Eventually, by tailoring our CTA to match the stage of the buyer's journey our audience was in, Facebook became one of our most effective channels —the leads just took longer since we had to wait for them to be ready to buy.

3. Event marketing

Event advertising is, basically, going to occasions to meet your possibilities face to face. Occasion promoting typically has a small bunch of various goals
- getting your item before possibilities, transforming gatherings with your possibilities into shut business, and meeting with existing arrangements to speed up deals velocity.

Event advertising keeps on being a main channel for B2B request gen advertisers. A recent report by Demand Gen Report observed that occasions were the
#1 best strategy for speeding up mid-and late-channel leads, and the
#3 strategy for connecting early-pipe leads.

On top of the income age targets, there are critical brand mindfulness helps that come from occasions. There are few other ways to get your brand in front of as many of your ideal client profile than at a trade show or conference—for the simple reason they're all in the same place at the same time.

Go to showcase groups ought to utilize occasions carefully. For instance, supporting an occasion for the most part requires a critical least offered, so "plunging a toe" and testing isn't a choice. In addition, occasions fall under the lightning strike model of advertising burning through a great deal of money, across the board spot to have a major effect. That implies according to a promoting point of view, occasions can be a hazardous mind-set. That is particularly obvious in the event that you're new to occasion marketing.

But don't allow this to deflect you. Assuming your industry has a solitary, strong occasion that you can hitch onto, then it very well may be a decent spot to send off your new item or solution.

Alternatively, occasions can shape some portion of your channel blend, to assemble mindfulness at the highest point of the pipe, take gatherings in the center, and speed up arrangements to close at the bottom.

How to get the most from events

Step 1: Choose your events carefully

Events address a gigantic venture for an organization, so you want to pick which occasions you go to painstakingly. This ought to basically be an activity like objective client work we examined earlier:

- Get a group of people breakdown from each significant occasion you're considering.
- See which level of participants are probably going to accommodate your objective audience.
- Use these to compute a good guess of the number of potential, top notch drives there are at the event.
- Apply your notable or projected transformation rates to ascertain a projected ROI.

Here's an illustration of this work, accepting a 20% MQL-SAL change rate and a 30% close rate:

Total # attendees	% attendees who fit your ICP	# potential leads	# MQLs you can expect	# closed deals you can expect
5,000	15	750	150	75

If you do this for each occasion, you'll get a feeling of how much return you can expect for your speculation. Taking a gander at potential MQLs additionally gives you a decent gauge to contrast every occasion with other non-occasion promoting channels.

Step 2: Define a goal for each event

Just like any other channel, events can be used to achieve different objectives: brand awareness, new opportunity creation, or existing pipeline acceleration.

You need to define a goal for every event so you understand how to measure success, as well as what lever you need to pull depending on where your go to market strategy is lagging.

Brand awareness vs events ROI

I used to work at a product startup. Whenever I joined, occasions were a major piece of their advertising blend, addressing the largest part of promoting spend. Nonetheless, whenever I dove into where open doors and arrangements were coming from, it was never from occasions. It shifted focus over to me like we were spending large cash on occasions, and not seeing a profit from that spend. But every time I tried to challenge the story that events are good, I was met with resistance. Ends up, it was justifiably. Since each time we went to an occasion, regardless of whether the actual occasion pay for itself, the effect on our image mindfulness was colossal. We'd get individuals coming dependent upon us and say "you all are all over!" By spending large at occasions, we had the option to make the deception of size and drive critical brand mindfulness among our ICP. The outcome was that we were continually being brought into bargains against our rivals who had raised countless dollars with outbound outreach groups of 50-100 reps.

4. Content marketing and SEO

Content marketing is all about creating content (videos, webinars, blog posts, white papers, ebooks, etc.) that your target audience finds helpful or interesting. The goal is to provide value so you can:

- Create the space to talk about your product or service.
- Provide value and build brand equity in your target audience, so that when they are looking, they know who to go to.

More strategically, happy showcasing completes two things.

In the first place, it makes content that individuals will utilize their contact data (generally an email address) to get sufficiently close to. When you have that contact data, you can market to them to check whether they need your item or administration. The white paper utilized before in our interest age crusade is a genuine illustration of this.

Second, by making on the web content like blog entries, content promoting supports your site's situation in Google list items. This implies that when your ideal interest group goes searching for replies to their concerns, your site is bound to appear in their list items, and they'll be bound to tap on your connection. When they do that, you have the chance to change over them into promoting caught drives (MCLs).

This subsequent undertaking is tied near website improvement, or SEO.

Website optimization is the specialty of getting what individuals are looking for and making the substance in light of those search questions. It's additionally the study of getting your substance to rank higher than everybody else.

There are many advisers for SEO, (Ahrefs, Brian Dean, and Moz SEO all have superb assets) so we won't get excessively granular here. But from a go to showcase viewpoint, there are a couple of things to call out.

- **Content marketing / SEO takes a long time**. While other channels like search engine or social media marketing can be quickly turned on and off, content takes a long time to generate and SEO takes a long time to work.

- **Content marketing / SEO has lower acquisition costs in the long run**. Not only do leads from organic search tend to convert at a higher rate, but they also cost less. Paid acquisition is a linear cost model—you need to spend more to get more, up to a certain point where spending more doesn't get you more. For content and SEO though, the initial cost of generating a piece of content can pay dividends for months or years. And because virtually the entire cost is up front, for every new lead that's acquired, your customer acquisition costs drops for that channel. Over time, this makes content marketing and SEO one of the most cost effective marketing channels today. Figure X.X shows what this looks like in practice.

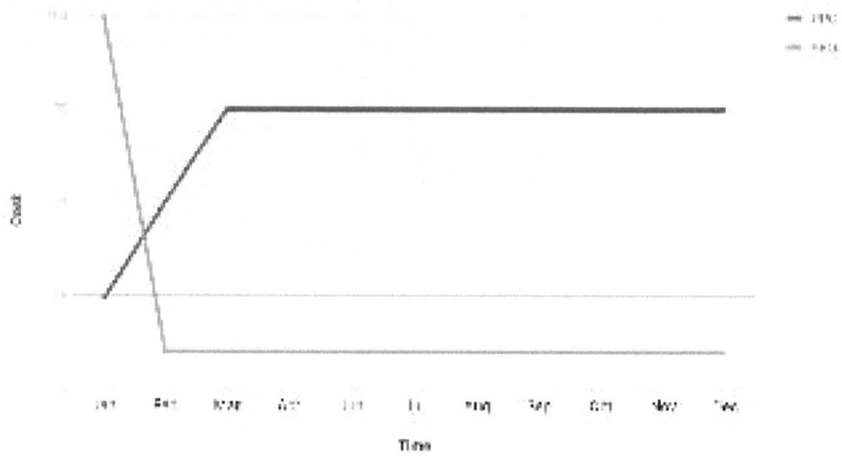

Keep your content customer-centric

It can be enticing to make content according to your point of view, as opposed to according to the point of view of your clients. For example, it's genuinely simple to split your substance up into segments in light of key item includes. But this isn't usually how customers think. They don't go through consistently fixating on your item and its capacities. All things being equal, they are investing their energy agonizing over things like how to develop their business, accelerate their interaction, or prevent clients from leaving.

So it is smart to put together your substance starting from the top, starting with client trouble spots and goals. Whenever you take care of those, you can present data about item includes that show that you can address each problem area and aspiration.

For instance, a title on your page could say: "Lessen stock carrying costs." Beneath this, you can talk about product features that help customers reduce inventory carrying costs, such as: "With our proprietary forecasting algorithm, you'll cut waste production by 33%."

On your website, it can be very helpful to have specific sections for each major customer group. This forces you write content in a customer-centric way rather than listing product details in an egocentric way.

Content examples

Webinars

Webinars-particularly ones that give instructive substance are perhaps the best method for getting clients. They're an extraordinary way for you to offer instructive worth to imminent clients, and they're a decent mechanism for giving specialized data about your item or administration. Hence, they can actually pull those possibilities still in the thought get rid of the woodwork, and they can assist you with speeding up bargains currently in motion.

You can advance your online course utilizing your email information base of leads. Make sure to be forceful here: you can convey numerous messages to get whatever number individuals to enlist as could be expected under the circumstances, and you ought to likewise make certain to send different update messages to guarantee that individuals who register really go to the occasion. Once the online course is finished, convey the recording and urge individuals to call or email to get more information.

There are a couple of things you can do to keep your crowd engaged:

1. Put surveys or inquiries into the content.
2. Try and fabricate a compatibility and get as much to and fro as possible.
3. Add in an overview toward the finish to assemble market insight to

sharpen your marketing.

4. Keep it short: 30 minutes is ideal, however 45 is you truly need more
    time.

Case studies

According to explore in Harvard Business Review, the contextual
investigation is the
single most perused piece of content that organizations produce. People are
social creatures. We are regular traditionalists who depend on friendly
evidence to approve our own way of behaving. And this makes case studies
extraordinarily powerful pieces of content marketing. They show that
somebody like your planned client has made progress utilizing your item or
service.

Case studies are especially powerful in the event that you can evaluate
results. Quantitative information assists your possibilities with getting the
wellspring of significant worth, and it gives them a really substantial, explicit
aspiration.

Case studies are additionally successful in light of the fact that they can be
utilized to recount to a convincing tale about your item or administration. As
indicated by the publicist Bob Bly, contextual investigations ought to be
composed like editorial articles-as opposed to delivering a dry examination,
recount to an interesting anecdote about how one client accomplished all that
they at any point longed for in view of your product.

To make the most out of your contextual investigations, attempt to get
as much happy as possible:

- Bring a videographer with you to interview the client in person and
  make a video case study
- Edit down the best bits to a 90-second video
- Get the best snippets for 10-15 second social media video ads
-

Turn the interview into a customer story page on your website

- Build a downloadable PDF case study that's longer and more detailed
- Run a webinar where you interview the client on what's been successful

Viral content

A ton of advertisers laugh at making viral substance as a component of a go to market methodology. They don't approach viral preparation in a serious way. We do.

We approach it in a serious way on the grounds that the examination on various client ventures recommends verbal exchange is the absolute most significant element. Individuals catch wind of items from others, so somehow, a decent advertiser should figure out how to drive expression of-mouth.

The second explanation we treat virality in a serious way is on the grounds that one of the top business colleges on the planet does. There is some not kidding research on viral advertising that is occurred at Wharton, the Ivy League business college at the University of Pennsylvania. Our establishment for viral showcasing comes from Wharton Professor Jonah Berger, writer of the book Contagious.

Here's the system for making viral substance, called the STEPPS structure. Each letter addresses an element in virality. I'll walk you through each of these:

- **Social currency**. People like to share things that make them look good to others. For example, you might share a company's video if it makes you look intelligent.

- **Triggers**. People share things when they are triggered to do so with reminders. For example, Irish products are likely to get shared on St Patrick's Day.

- ◢ *Emotion*. People share things that are emotionally arousing. Content that makes us angry or uplifted are likely to energize us to take action and share it.

- ◢ *Public*. When something is public, it is far more likely to spread than something that is private. For example, an Apple laptop with a visible logo is more likely to spread than a laptop with no logo on it.

- ◢ *Practical value*. Things that provide practical, useful information are likely to get shared. For example, a tip sheet on buying a new home will likely get shared with a friend who is looking to buy a new home.

- ◢ *Stories*. People tend to think more in terms of narratives than in terms of facts. Embedding a brand message in a story with a beginning, middle, and end is more likely to be remembered and shared than a list of benefits.

5. Email marketing

Despite tireless cases that "email is dead," it keeps on being a staggeringly compelling interest age strategy for both B2B and B2C channels. It's financially savvy and quick to convey, and it can assume a solid supporting part for other interest gen strategies like substance marketing.

The essential thought of email promoting is to convey messages to your ideal interest group, consequently and throughout an extensive stretch of time (called a "trickle crusade") to keep your image top of psyche, teach them on the issue you settle, and attempt to motivate them to change over to a lead or a client with convincing offers or calls to action.

There are 4 normal dribble crusades that apply to both B2B and B2C organizations. Which mission style you pick will rely upon the assets, refinement, and tech stack that you approach. All things considered, recollect: there could be no silver slug in advertising and this goes for email showcasing too. Assuming you have the limit, attempt different procedures and look at results at the end.

Email newsletter drip campaign

This is by a long shot the simplest mission to construct and send. An email bulletin as a rule comprises of a couple of content pieces that you've created, some industry-important news, and maybe some report about your business. On the off chance that you're a B2C organization, the pamphlet is normally a chance to show what new items or updates you have, and an opportunity to offer some sort of markdown. Email pamphlets typically go out to the whole client base, and you can smooth out this interaction by utilizing a device like Mailchimp.

Audience-based drip campaign

Audience-based trickle crusades are email crusades that section your ideal interest group by what their identity is. For instance, say you're a B2B business who sells a mind boggling item with heaps of purchasers associated with the interaction. You might separate out your buying committee into different personas, then serve them different content based on who they are and what your value proposition means to them. According to a B2C point of view, this would be like dividing in light of segment data, for instance a web based business clothing organization serving ladies' garments to ladies and men's garments to men.

Since crowd particulars are typically genuinely fixed, this can be executed with basic programming like Mailchimp.

Content-based drip campaign

Content-based dribble crusades are planned so you have various trickle crusades, every one zeroing in on satisfied from an alternate item, worth, or topic. Clients are added to a high level "content blender" crusade, which has content from each sub-dribble. Whenever a client answers one of the expert blender messages, they're diverted so they then get served more happy like the substance they drew in with.

Content mixer campaign

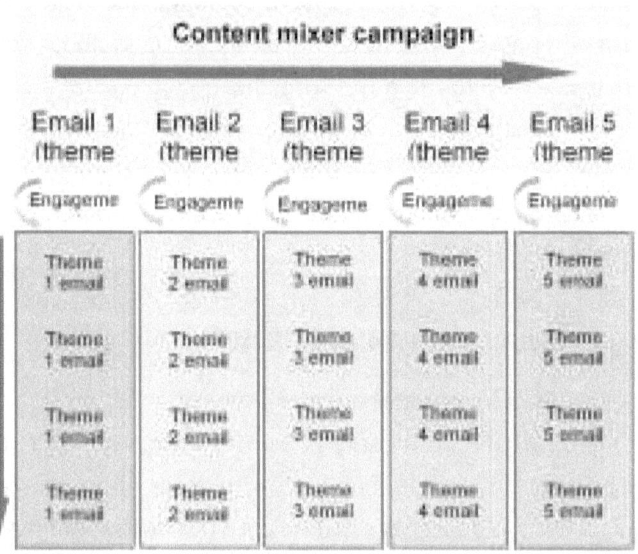

Content-based trickles are more convoluted than crowd and pamphlets, for the straightforward explanation that who gets what email-and what you're basing that on
- changes over the long haul. In any case, they will generally have
better commitment, Since you're putting together each new email with respect to what worked successfully previously. Since
content-based dribbles are intricate to execute, you'll typically have to utilize devices like HubSpot, Pardot, Marketo, or Eloqua.

Intent-based drip campaigns

The last sort of trickle crusade is plan based dribble crusades. Here, each new email that you ship off a particular possibility depends on their past commitment with your business. This commitment may be a site visit, past email opens or snaps, tapping on an advertisement, or perusing/watching/consuming/downloading your content.

In the B2C world, intent-based campaigns work well if you can retarget users based on the products they were looking at and didn't purchase. In the B2B world, intent-based campaigns can form a crucial part of your lead qualification process by serving content that is relevant to the particular point that the prospect is at in their decision process. Operationally, this is usually done with lead scoring. Users with a low score might be served content focused on educating them about the problem you solve. Those with higher scores might get emails that focus on quantifying the value of your solution (e.g. with an ROI calculator).

Don't let perfect be the enemy of good

Marketers often get analysis paralysis when they try to figure out how best to maximize their email efforts. I always chuckle when I hear people talk about the perfect time to send an email. The common wisdom is that Tuesday morning is somehow the optimal time to send out business emails. But I have also seen research suggesting that click-through rates are particularly high on weekends, even though open rates tend to be lower.

People have an odd fixation with the science of email timing—and they buy into the myth that there's a perfect time to get their email out the door. But —controversial opinion—I don't think it's all that important when you send your emails. The timing of your email send should be trumped by the *actual value that your emails provide*. Deciding whether to mention pain point A or B in your email is far more important than whether you send it at 11 a.m. Pacific or 11 a.m. Eastern time.

Marketers likewise invest a great deal of energy stressing over culminating the designs in an email. But I've seen research from HubSpot that suggests that plain text emails actually perform better than graphic emails—even though they take a tiny fraction of the time to produce. I've likewise seen essential messages delivered in Outreach perform well, despite the fact that they don't have illustrations at all.

Customers regularly view fundamental messages like they were coming from a companion. While excessively smooth messages can have an atmosphere of persuasiveness that switches clients off. The reality: fixating on plan frequently does not merit the effort.

It is impossible that your promoting will be productive to such an extent that the additional dollars you gain from advancing your email send time or your illustrations will merit the time it takes to do that. You're vastly improved investing energy making your incentive more grounded or fixing your crowd division. So-don't let the ideal be the adversary of the upside. And don't let the small details trump the big picture of your overall marketing strategy.

6. Display ads

Display ads are things like banner ads, YouTube pre-roll ads, and text ads that appear on websites other than your own. Depending on which ad network you choose, these can be priced per click (e.g. PPC), per 1,000 impressions, or CPM.

Generally, show advertisements are just successful as a brand mindfulness strategy. That is on the grounds that their active visitor clicking percentage is far lower than channels like Facebook or LinkedIn. But they're often very inexpensive to run, and they allow you to retarget users from your website or email campaigns. For your interest group, this can make the feeling that your image is wherever as though you sent off a major, costly brand mindfulness crusade, when actually you are spending pennies per impression.

7. **Direct mail**

That's right, old-school, physical, post office based mail. Your regular postal mail could take a couple of structures: postcards printed from Postcardmania; transcribed notes created and sent by administrations like Sendoso for an individual touch; bundles that incorporate things like chocolates or merch.

Used well, regular postal mail can produce quick outcomes. For example, you can utilize post office based mail to stand out (perhaps by offering a free item or preliminary) and afterward rapidly secure a gathering through a subsequent email. Post office based mail is likewise successful assuming your interest group is joined by topography. For instance, assuming that you're going to a gathering in Texas, you could send standard mail advancements to individuals in your CRM who live in Texas.

One illustration of this comes from when I worked at a huge UK-based bank and protection supplier. I dealt with the advertising group for pet protection, and regular postal mail was a major piece of our promoting blend. The explanation we depended on this is that we had the option to distinguish explicit postcodes around the UK that over-ordered for pet people (that is, assuming you thumped on 100 entryways in that postcode, a more prominent possibility of the inhabitant was being an animal person than if you thumped on 100 irregular entryways the nation over). This made our post office based mail practical, and subsequently gave us a decent profit from investment.

8. **All the others...**

There are, obviously, loads of different strategies that you can add to your munitions stockpile. These incorporate out of home, conventional media, natural online entertainment, force to be reckoned with promoting, and then some. And if you can layer these into your demand mix and they make financial sense, that's great. But for most go to market plans, the 7 tactics listed above will get you most of the way there.

Brand vs demand marketing

Brand promoting is regularly introduced as something contrary to request showcasing. In brand advertising, the story goes, estimation doesn't make any difference everything revolves around narrating and ethereal brand building. In all actuality, however, brand advertising is a channel like some other. It has measurements and targets. It's only not as simple to connect the advertising dollars you spend to the income dollars you make.

Brand promoting is essentially centered around establishing however many positive connections as could be allowed to expand your image value that is, the worth your image brings to your association. A positive brand value can be incredibly strong. For instance, Apple's image value is a major piece of why they can charge large number of dollars for an iPhone. Positive brand value can likewise go about as a type of protection. Assuming that your appearance is tainted in any capacity, your positive image value can help fight off a drop in revenue.

Brand promoting is additionally centered around brand mindfulness. For the most part, brand mindfulness is a proportion of whether individuals know your image. However, there are various ways of characterizing and measure it.

The most grounded approach's called independent brand mindfulness. This implies individuals can name your image with next to no kind of prompts. For instance, you could ask a purchaser, "What extravagance half and half vehicles would you be able to name?" They could say Lexus, Lincoln, and Cadillac. That is uplifting news for you on the off chance that you're showcasing for Lincoln since you've quite recently demonstrated that somewhere around somebody has independent familiarity with your brand.

Another famous methodology is helped mindfulness. This is the place where you, as the economic specialist, give a rundown of brands or prompts. For instance, in a study you could inquire "Which of the accompanying brands have you known about?" If

they mark off your image, then you've exhibited that they have known about your image. This isn't so dependable as independent mindfulness, however it's more straightforward to gauge and place into surveys.

If you're chipping away at huge brands, you'll probably get your image mindfulness information from an outsider like Nielsen. Nielsen is one of the main statistical surveying organizations, and they give programming to follow such KPIs. They routinely direct examination with clients to gather this data.

If you're working for a little organization, you likely will not approach such an information without any problem. You might have to send reviews out to irregular individuals inside your objective client gathering to assist you with getting a best guess of your image mindfulness. One of the upsides of doing your own reviews is that you get exceptionally applicable information. Instead of getting information from the overall population, you'll gather information inside your profoundly significant objective gathering of people. You can then quantify your image mindfulness over the long haul to check progress.

There are other, more indirect approaches to assessing brand mindfulness, for example, taking a gander at scan information for your image on Google's watchword planner.

Here you can see that Mountain Dew has a normal inquiry volume somewhere in the range of 100K and 1 million.

Brand	Yuppies	Deal-seekers	Practical buyers
A	30%	11%	5%

B	2%	11%	12%
C	3%	3%	8%
D	1%	19%	3%

Often what we're keen on is brand mindfulness by every one of the brands on the lookout (counting our own and our rivals') and furthermore by every one of the significant client bunches in the market.

Here you can see that one of our client fragments, called Yuppies, is especially mindful of brand A yet really unaware of different brands. On the off chance that we own image A, we can see an unmistakable benefit here. Brand B is notable in the two different sections. As an advertising specialist, this data is exceptionally valuable. Brand A could benefit by publicizing more to Deal-searchers. Brand D could benefit by supporting mindfulness among Deal-searchers as well.

Brand mindfulness and brand advertising, generally speaking, include large, costly missions, and are typically more qualified to develop items further along the item lifecycle.

When brands do and do not matter

I saw an intriguing inquiry on Quora as of late: a client was contemplating whether brands become more significant the more the item resembles a ware. It's a fascinating inquiry, and we can involve it as a leaping off highlight show when and where brands assume a huge part in promoting and, perhaps more significantly, when they truly don't. This is essential to dive into in light of the fact that I've seen an excessive number of organizations put vigorously in marking that truly yields no outcomes. This segment will assist you with deciding if marking ought to be vital in your go to showcase strategy.

First, how about we check out at a few items. Take more time for example.

Here, marking doesn't exactly make any difference. Organizations will purchase rock paying little mind to what

brand name is slapped on it. Presently ponder ketchup. Ketchup is an item as well, however here marking really matters a lot. In this way, we have two products where the job of marking is very different.

Now we should consider something not a ware. Take a Rolls Royce, for instance. Here, marking is critical for driving purchases.

Okay, so what's going on here? To comprehend, we really want to separate this. The best spot to begin is with the 7 showcasing strategies that make esteem on the lookout. These are:

1. Products
2. Brands
3. Services
4. Prices
5. Communications
6. Incentives
7. Distribution

With wares like rock, the actual item doesn't actually make esteem. That is on the grounds that it is indistinct from the contenders' items. So-on the off chance that the item isn't making the worth, does that mean the brand needs to?

Now and again that is valid, yet not dependably. Recollect our rock model above, where we discovered that marking doesn't exactly make any difference for selling this essential commodity.

So, to truly unload how brands make esteem, we want to go a level further. Basically, there are three different ways that brands can make value:

1. They make utilitarian worth, for example, imparting the nature of the

product.

2. They make mental worth, for example, depicting your character through dress labels.
3. Lastly, they make financial worth, for example, conveying the cost positioning.

With business-to-business commodities such as gravel, the psychological value of the brand doesn't really matter. Nor does the utilitarian or money related esteem. On the off chance that you have an item where brand doesn't make any of these qualities, emptying time and assets into marking won't be valuable.

But with business-to-consumer commodities such as ketchup or corn flakes, the brand actually *does* create psychological value. Whenever the individual eats corn drops, the actual brand affects the eating experience. You may really partake in the item more since it was marked in a certain way.

The main concern: brands matter more in settings where they can make practical, mental, and financial value.

How to build great ad creative

There's no single formula for building great ad creative, but there are three major approaches that you can consider.

When I worked on TV ads, the approach I used—and the one I recommend—was developed by the acclaimed Leo Burnett advertising agency. It's called "The Big Idea." You focus on a single benefit, and then highlight attributes that support that benefit. In other words, you communicate one benefit, but you provide prospective customers with multiple reasons to believe in that benefit.

The inverse of this is talking about multiple benefits and a single attribute that creates those benefits. For example, automation might lead to lower labor costs, faster processing, and reduced wait times.

A third methodology is narrating. This one is acquiring a great deal of footing in the business world today. People for the most part think regarding accounts, so we can undoubtedly review promotions that fit a characteristic story. With this methodology, you regularly need to introduce your item or your proposal as the legend of the story.

Many organizations will as of now have a plan for how to do promotions. But advances marketers need to know the right time to use the right approach. To dive more deeply into these methodologies (and when they're generally valuable), I'd propose perusing Advertising Strategy by Brian Sternthal and Derek Rucker. But here is a quick and dirty guide:

- **Approach 1**, where you focus on a single benefit, is a good approach when you have a single benefit with lots of attributes to support it. For example, Volvo is safe because it has airbags, a collision warning system, and a blind spot information system.

- **Approach 2**, where you focus on multiple benefits, is best where you have a very specific, unique attribute that offers your prospective customers a whole host of benefits. Our automation example applies again here: automation increases speed and accuracy, which in turn saves your customers' time, money and other resources

- **Approach 3**, storytelling, works best when it's important to *demonstrate* the benefit(s). For example, it might work best when it's difficult to convey the value of the product without showing a case study. Storytelling also works well if the product has some kind of emotional or psychological value.

Of course, there are other creative strategies that can work in certain situations. For example, if your product has a very strong point of difference, you could simply communicate that buying the product will yield a particular benefit. This aggressive approach can work if the product is unique.

Or, if your product is complicated, analogies can be much better at communicating value than any other creative approach, because they allow you to relate something your prospects don't understand to something with which they're already familiar or comfortable.

Chapter summary questions

- Have you clarified the demand generation process, including definitions and responsibilities, with the go to market team?
- Have you identified your target demand tactics and developed, hired, or outsourced capabilities in each?
- Have you identified key tactics for every stage of the demand generation funnel?
- Is branding going to be a key part of your marketing strategy?

PART 6:
THE IT IS CHANGING TO MARKET MIX
How to measure channel effectiveness

Marketing. All things considered, we've lived in an inventory driven world. That implies that supply was low and request was high, so organizations had a ton of force. They zeroed in on the production network, since the essential concern was getting an adequate number of units assembled and transported to fulfill need. This is basically the account of mid-century America.

Interestingly, we currently live in an interest driven world. Purchasers hold the vast majority of the power, and they can request that providers take care of their particular necessities. This is the thing The Cambridge Group alludes to as the "request chain" instead of the "production network." In this new interest driven world, choices have detonated; needs are explicit, as opposed to conventional; and the assumption is that those particular requirements are met in a particular and designated manner. On top of these changes, clients do a huge load of examination all alone, especially right off the bat in the purchasing stage. This implies that B2B advertisers need to adjust and meet clients where they arc in the purchasing cycle. The equivalent is valid in B2C, where clients go to audits to survey products.

Because of these changes, go to advertise groups can never again bear to depend only on some channel. Rather, in an undeniably aggressive world, the best way to effectively go to advertise is to do as such across different showcasing channels on the double, and to depend on the total effect being more noteworthy than the amount of its parts.

So, accomplishing the right promoting blend is a urgent component in any go to showcase process. In this part, we will do a profound plunge into the promoting blend, looking at:

- How to calculate your marketing mix
- A guide to planning out your marketing mix in Excel
- An example of an integrated marketing campaign

Marketers frequently play top choices, supporting one showcasing strategy over another. Be that as it may, you can't allow your inclination to hinder the development objectives of your business.

Here's a model. I'm inclined toward pay-per-click watchword advertisements and points of arrival. I particularly like Unbounce because it allows me to quickly create landing pages and test key features such as the header text and the hero image (that is, the main image on a web page, landing page, or ad). I likewise love utilizing Google's catchphrase organizer. I was ensured in Adwords and I esteem the convenient, quantitative data.

But by and large, this kind of quantitative, test advanced promoting isn't the most fitting methodology. In proficient administrations advertising, for instance, public talking is doubtful the best strategy. In this way, advertisers need a level of modesty and adaptability with senses of judgment to accomplish development objectives. On the off chance that I was working in proficient administrations promoting and continually pushing pay-per-click catchphrase advertisements over open speaking, I wouldn't take care of my business. But I also wouldn't be doing my job if I *only* focused on public speaking— creating an effective marketing mix is generally even more important than identifying the most effective stand-alone approach.

Luckily, there's an interaction that permits you to eliminate inclination from your strategic direction. It's called media-blend demonstrating. It utilizes statistical

regressions to identify the ideal mix of different media such as TV, PPC, SEO, etc. Here's how it's done.

Calculating the media mix

You can do media-blend displaying yourself utilizing Excel, Stata, SPSS, or another measurable program. However, working out the ideal media blend can get pretty convoluted. We should begin with a basic example.

	F	G	H	I	J	K
		sales	tv	print	ppc	seo
year 1		20	5	2	1	0.5
year 2		25	6	3	2	1
year 3		15	2	1	0.5	0.3

This table shows a record of deals across three years. It additionally shows how much was spent on every medium in every year. In year 1, five million was spent on TV, 2 million was spent on print, 1 million was spent on pay-per-click advertising (PPC), and half a million was spent on search-engine optimization (SEO).

Here's the manner by which you'd do your media-blend advertising in with this data:

1. Click the information tab in Excel and go to Data Analysis on the extreme right. On the off chance that this choice isn't accessible, you really want to add the Excel include for information analysis.
2. Select Regression starting from the drop and snap OK.
3. For the y-range, select the sales column. For the x-range, select the columns for TV, print, etc. Then press OK.

	Coefficients	Standard Error	t Stat	P-value	Lower 95%	Upper 95%	Lower 95.0%	Upper 95.0%
Intercept	11	0	55525	#NUM!	11	11	11	11
TV	1	0	55555	#NUM!	1	1	1	1
print	0	0	55535	#NUM!	0	0	0	0
ppc	4	0	55555	#NUM!	4	4	4	4
seo	0	0	55535	#NUM!	0	0	0	0

This is what your result resembles. Note that PPC has a coefficient of 4 and TV has a coefficient of 1. This lets you know that PPC and TV are the best indicator of deals. So to increment deals, you ought to focus your spending plan here.

This was an exceptionally fundamental examination. As an advertiser, you'd by and large depend on your investigation accomplices to assist you with growing more refined models.

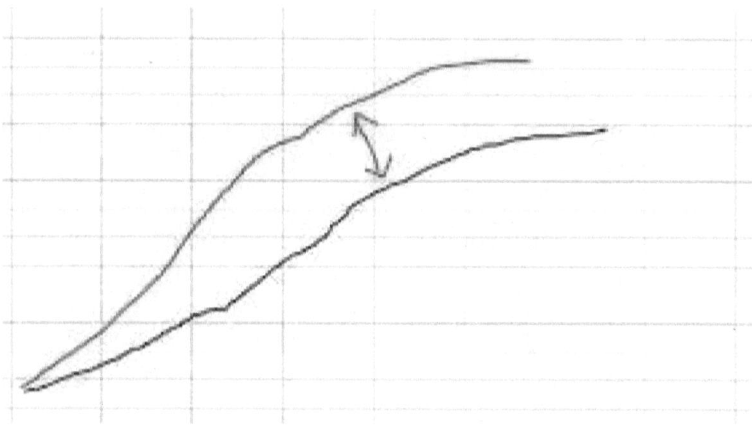

In this chart, I am showing deals on the upward hub and time on the right pivot. In further developed models, what you would do is lay out a base case. My base case here is the blue line. The blue line shows the forecast of deals assuming I didn't spend anything on media (this would represent existing force and irregularity). The red line demonstrates the anticipated deals by spending on media. Along these lines, what we're truly intrigued by according to an administration viewpoint is the space shown by the red bolts. This is the genuine effect of media.

Two issues you may run into

When you are investigating such an information, there are two normal issues that you could run into.

The first is that not each of your information will be quantitative. For instance, male and female are not measurements. In cases like these, first think about whether those variables are even too significant. Frequently advertisers overemphasize segment information when truth be told, persuasive or attitudinal information is more significant. Second, consider treating the information with faker factors. For instance, 0 could mean male and 1 could mean female.

The second issue you might run into is comparing data with different scales. For example, you might have miles, pounds, dollars, inches, etc. The key to addressing these differences is to standardize the data before you start running statistical analyses. That could look something like this:

Original data	Standardized data
1km	3.57
2km	0.71

Average = 1.5

Standard deviation = 0.7

This is a straightforward method for normalizing the information. In this model, we have two relevant informative items: 1km and 2km. For every relevant informative item, deduct the mean for the dataset and afterward partition by the standard deviation of the dataset. Presently we have two normalized elements, and we can contrast these new normalized information with other datasets that could have pounds, dollars, inches, etc.

Building your marketing mix

At this point in the go to showcase process, you know your crowd, your offer, and you have a smart thought of your advertising request channels.
You know if brand will be essential for your blend, and you've done a huge load of work on crowd definition, esteem creation, and messaging.
Now, it's opportunity to lay everything out in a promoting blend. Your promoting blend is the particular conveyance of spend across channels, resources, and time. Fundamentally, what cash is going where, and when.

Triggers vs the funnel

Old-school advertisers consider the client choices venture as a straight way, starting with mindfulness and finishing off with buy. This is the exemplary channel, and it's served go to advertise groups for years.

But as of late, McKinsey fostered a more complex system that recommends that the it isn't direct to purchase venture. Rather, it's really founded on triggers. *Triggers are key minutes that impel the purchasing process.*

For instance, an organization could begin investigating new programming when they arrive at a specific size and their the norm begins to separate. Or then again somebody could begin investigating for contract programming while they're searching for another loft or going through a separation. These triggers are unimaginably significant in light of the fact that they are articulation focuses: they're minutes when you can infuse your item into the conversation and become exceptionally relevant.

With that as a top priority, you ought to recall triggers while you're thinking about your advertising blend. Your blend ought to point to:

1. Accelerate when those triggers surface for your objective customers
2. Educate prospects about those triggers
3. Create content that solves the pain those triggers have surfaced
4. Develop processes and drip campaigns that quickly take prospects from vaguely interested to ready to buy.

How to build a marketing calendar

Building a mission expects you to work across numerous advertising channels immediately (as opposed to depending on a solitary showcasing strategy to do everything). And in order to do that, you need to develop a way to stay organized, and to keep all of your departments on the same page.

I've chipped away at numerous intricate showcasing efforts, incorporating worldwide item dispatches with multi-million dollar financial plans, and I can let you know that when you manage various moving parts, you want an iron-clad authoritative procedure. In any case, the entire thing spins out of control, fast.

Here's the manner by which I suggest putting together your advertising mix:

1. Start with an accounting sheet like Google Sheets or Microsoft Excel. Google Sheets is by and large better, since you can work together and share it progressively. Like that, everybody in your organization is in total agreement literally.
2. Make the upward pivot of your bookkeeping sheet the kinds of showcasing resources. In this way, the main section ought to comprise of resource classes: for instance, cell 2 may be "recordings," cell 3 may be "print," and cell 4 may be "banners."
3. Make the even hub time, so your subsequent segment may be "week 1," the third segment "week 2, etc. It is useful to likewise bundle these into months.

Asset Categories	Week 1	Week 2
videos		
print		
banners		

Once you have this structure set up, you can begin entering the different showcasing things you will utilize. Here, it's useful to utilize shading coding:

- Blue might mean "finished"

- Green might mean "released" (note: it's important to distinguish between when an item is expected to be finished and when it is actually released to the market)
- Reserve red for red-flag issues such as delays

From here, there are different layers of intricacy that you could add. For instance, the main tab could connect with Product 1 though another tab could connect with Product 2. The primary portion of your sheet may be for one area while the base half connects with another. Basically you can change this overall layout to the particular necessities of your company.

Then, the main thing left to do is to really populate your promoting schedule with your channels and assets!

Integrated vs discrete marketing

The most productive method for getting clients is through coordinated crusades not discrete channel exercises. Logical masterminds like to break things into parts and measure the exhibition of every one of those parts. On the off chance that Facebook is producing low procurement costs and LinkedIn isn't, you would normally need to siphon more cash into Facebook. But this approach is overly simplistic.

You have huge loads of touchpoints with a client at different stages in the client purchasing cycle. They generally don't choose to purchase from you due to one Google promotion or in light of one online entertainment post. And in situations where that is actually the case, your customer acquisition cost was probably too high. That is on the grounds that specific channels are more productive at creating mindfulness (like standard promotions with an extremely minimal expense for each impression).

Other missions are great at creating reactions to begin the discussion. These are things like Google promotions and presentation pages. But if you're expecting your Google ads to generate awareness, consideration, and purchase, then you're probably being very inefficient. In confinement, your information may be letting you know that Google advertisements have the least client procurement cost, yet taking a gander at the master plan, you really want to think in a more incorporated way.

By coordinating efforts and stricturing each channel and resource for just do what it's great at, you can amplify your showcasing spend and your promoting sway, without expanding your budget.

Lightning strike marketing

Agile approaches to management are very much in vogue right now, and

agile marketing is no exception. The idea is that you test and learn, pivoting as needed based on (1) the data you acquire through testing, and (2) how the market reacts to your marketing.

The advertising blend that we just illustrated mirrors this, building channels and testing over the long run. But there are times when you just need to go big or go home. In media outlets, for instance, it frequently appears to be legit to consolidate your advertising into an exceptionally short time span. That implies consuming the vast majority of your promoting financial plan close to the time you send off your product.

The test with amusement items is that your opposition is gigantic. Say, for instance, that you're showcasing a film. Your opposition isn't simply different films. It's not even other diversion items like computer games or books. It's every one of the many substitutes that the market offers your forthcoming clients, such as investing energy with family at the pool, or going on a climb, or taking a cooking class. Along these lines, to get seen, you really want to place every one of your assets into a concentrated attack. Entertainment showcasing resembles sending off a rocket transport. You don't fly a couple of feet in the air every day; all things considered, you set all your focus on one monster send off so you produce sufficient speed to get through the opposition of the environment. With diversion promoting, you're attempting to get through the clamor and mess to catch individuals' advantage and get them into the theater (or onto your membership service).

The protected methodology of trying things out to a great extent, improving consistently, simply doesn't produce sufficient power. With entertainment products such as movies and video games, the lion's share of revenue is generated in the short time just after the product is released to the market. The send off is so basic to progress in light of the fact that the income curve quickly trails off afterwards.

So, what does this mean for marketers whose products don't fall into the entertainment category? In most cases, you'll be going to market for the long term—and in that case, you're probably aiming for returns over a long, sustained period of time. But, you may still choose to do a lightning strike marketing strategy if you want to jumpstart your product launch.

An integrated campaign example

Let me walk you through an illustration of a really incorporated crusade intended to obtain new clients. I'll utilize a business-to-business model, however the standards can be applied to B2C as well.

Your initial step will probably be to purchase a rundown of target organizations. This is a significant advance that numerous advertisers miss: they begin running promotions, yet they haven't really characterized the universe of clients they need to gain. You can (and ought to) thin down precisely which clients you need to procure by working with a rundown specialist or a data set supplier. On the off chance that you're searching for an overall rundown supplier, you can go with an organization like InfoUSA; assuming you're searching for a specialty information base supplier, focus on an organization like Etail Insights. There are additionally organizations, as Leadium, that will incorporate records from scratch.

You can test different rundown suppliers to sort out which one yields the best. To test your rundowns, send precisely the same email to two records utilizing a program like Marketo. Whichever rundown delivers more qualified leads is the winner.

Once you've procured a rundown of target clients, your following stage is to run and test lead gen promotions. Run lead age promotions exactly to the gathering on your rundown and no other person. Would you be able to perceive how proficient this is? Rather than broadcasting to the world, your telecom barely to a predefined set of target customers.

Facebook and LinkedIn are two of the most remarkable stages to do this. They offer lead-generation ads that you can use to promote offers such as ebooks, free consultations, or free demos. Is that right: how could I pay to get somebody to download a free digital book? Indeed, the response to

this question connections direct about having a coordinated mission. In confinement, paying somebody to download a digital book would be idiotic. But in the context of an integrated campaign, it starts to make a lot of sense. The advertisement could create a digital book download, yet the subsequent channels could land the genuine deal. For instance, you could send ten messages to every individual who downloaded the digital book. The seventh email could incite individuals to purchase from you, or possibly address a sales rep. Collapsing in regular postal mail can be significant here as well.

So, now, you're hitting your possibilities with promotions and maybe post office based mail. You can likewise hit them with instructive messages that sustain the leads. Ordinarily these are instructive messages that offer some incentive to possibilities. You can send these naturally through Marketo, InfusionSoft, AWebber, Hubspot, MailChimp, or one of the robotization contributions from Salesforce. These are your overall advertising messages.

You can likewise utilize a program like Outreach to request possibilities with messages from your outbound outreach group. These will more often than not have a more private, 1-on-1 slant to them.

While all of this is going on, you could likewise be running general brand mindfulness standards on Facebook, LinkedIn, and Google. Re-focusing on site guests with standard advertisements can likewise be effective.

The thought here is that you're not depending on a solitary channel to create results. You're hitting similar rundown of possibilities with various channels either all the while or consecutively. This is an effective framework for getting new customers.

Chapter summary questions

- Have you planned out your marketing calendar?
- Have you secured executive buy-in for a mixed-channel approach to marketing?
- Are you pursuing a lightning strike approach to your product launch?
- Do you know what your audience triggers are, and do you know how to use different channels to deliver the right message at the right time?

PART 7:
HOW MUCH? ESTIMATING YOUR PRODUCT

Pricing is perhaps the most difficult component of the go to advertise technique. It's a harmony between charging to the point of meeting income assumptions and cover costs, while being low an adequate number of that clients get a positive profit from speculation for the worth you're promising. In this segment we will cover a portion of the normal valuing procedures, gotchas, and a couple of tips to augment your income with pricing.

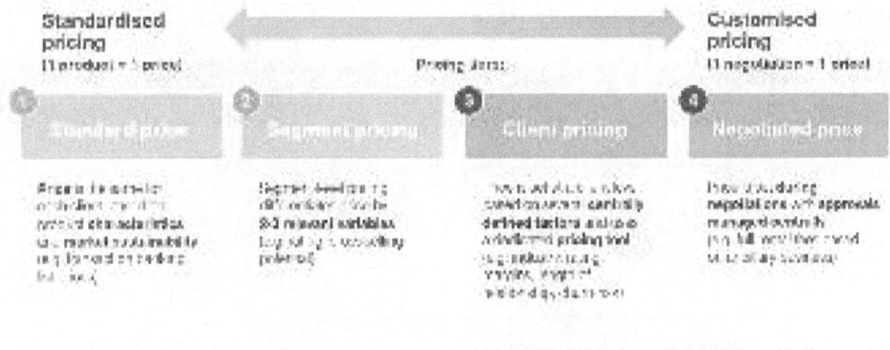

The ultimate pricing model is based on one or more pricing dimensions, product characteristics and target clients

Reference: Simon Kucher and Partners

This estimating model is planned explicitly for programming. Yet, most items can end up along the hub somewhere.

The fundamental thought behind this graph is that evaluating ought to have multiple
aspects. These aspects which are basically the factors that sway the cost
are usually:

1. Product dimensions
2. Usage dimensions
3. Volume dimensions
4. Client/contract dimensions

It's actually important that regularly, extremely straightforward items will just have one aspect. For instance, when I proceed to purchase a pack of kumquats, I follow through on a set cost. It doesn't make any difference assuming I purchase 100 packs (volume aspect), or then again in the event that I'm anticipating making a kumquat stew versus a kumquat salad, or how regularly I shop at the store.

Beyond this, the principal aspect to be added is quite often item. For instance, here's my hairdresser's valuing page:

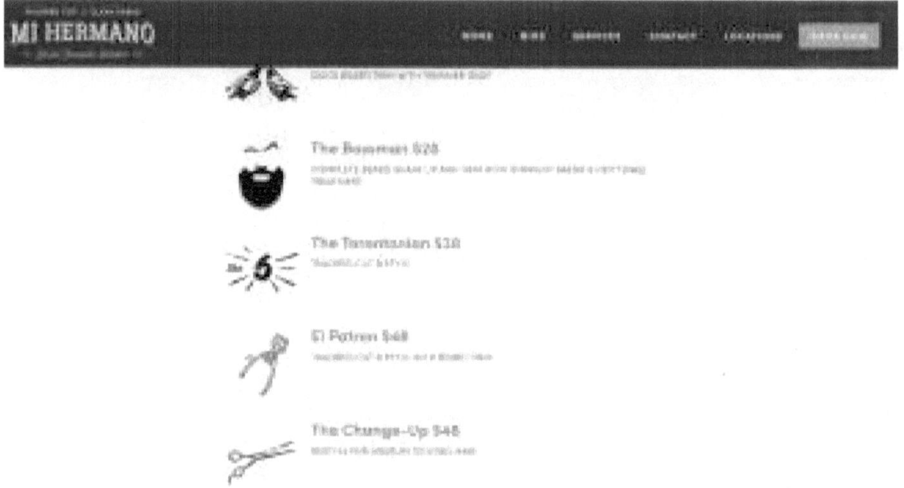

Their pricing list shows that as you spend more, you get more services (e.g. if you pay $10 more, you get a facial hair growth trim).

As items get more mind boggling, nonetheless, more aspects enter the condition. For basic B2C and some SMB-centered B2B programming, for instance, the standard aspects are item includes, with use and agreement length (month to month or yearly) layered on top.

Zapier, for instance, involves use as an essential switch for valuing. Their most minimal level is free, yet you just get 5 destroys and 100 errands each month. As you stir up the levels, they begin to present more factors and the quantity of destroys and errands increments, All things considered, the quality stays the equivalent it's just the volume of item you get that changes.

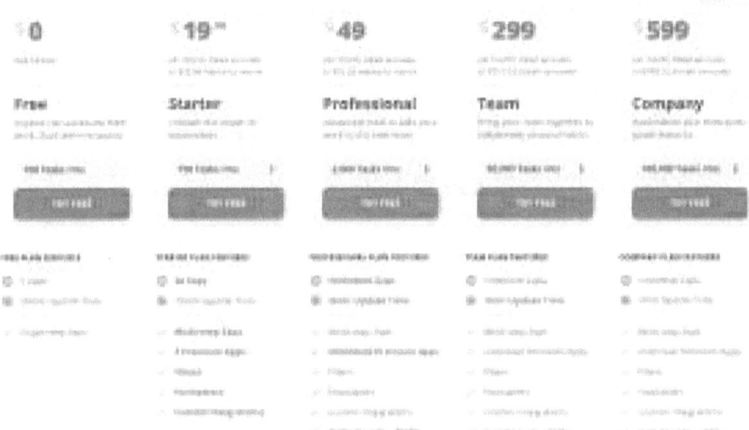

Amazon prime, conversely, is estimated exclusively founded on agreement length:

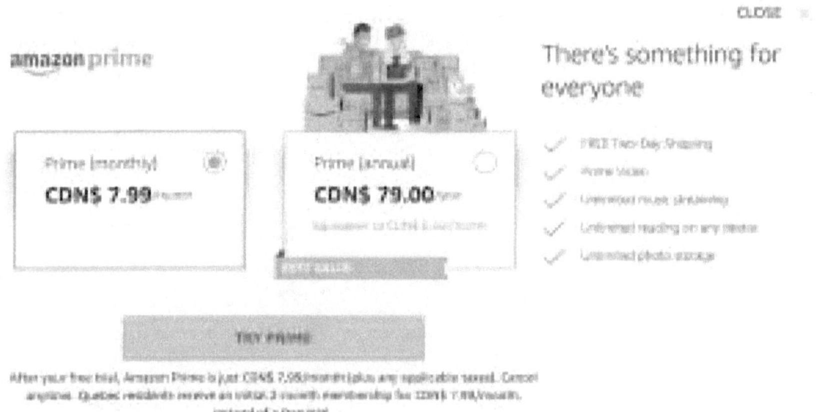

Their cost goes somewhere near 17% assuming you sign a yearly contract.

As items get more convoluted, you start to see factors assembled into significant cans. The ideal estimating structure has something like one of every one of these aspects, with the limits set to focus on a particular use case.

If we look again at Zapier's valuing page, they've worked really hard of marking their evaluating plans to engage various portions of their crowd. Assuming I'm an organization searching for an API association instrument, I know precisely where to go. In like manner, in the event that I'm a one-individual activity and I simply need my email to associate with a Google sheet, I know exactly where to go as well.

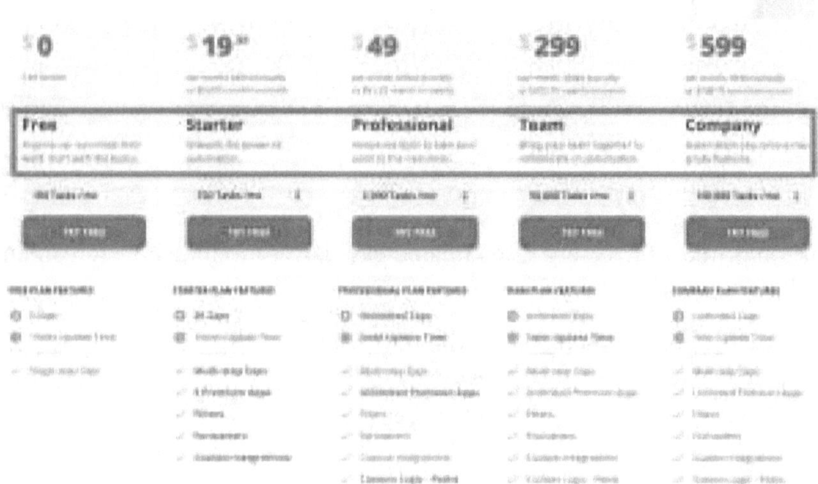

If executed accurately, layered evaluating techniques like this should:

- Provide value to the user equal to the price they're paying.
- Push users to upgrade to a higher tier as they begin to extract more value from the product.
- Allow you to sell the same underlying product at different price points based on the value that your customer is going to get (e.g. with Zapier, a company automating 100,000 tasks a month is getting a lot more value than a freelancer automating 750 tasks a month).
- Reward longer contracts (since an annual up-front contract is effectively a loan) with better pricing, while also reducing churn (since customers have already paid for a year they'll be stickier).

On top of these factors, obviously, is the job valuing plays in dealings. Limiting, long term bargains, good installment terms, and more are altogether switches that salesmen can pull to finalize a negotiation. Be that as it may, the center fundamental construction of multi-faceted evaluating stays in civility and

is (as we would like to think) the most ideal way to convey greatest worth to a scope of clients at a scope of prices.

Your price needs to align with your goal

Let's say you need to produce $1,000,000 MRR and you're presently at $200,000 with 2,000 clients. How about we likewise say that your objective client bunch has a populace of 4,000. Regardless of whether each and every client in the market was a client of yours, you'd just be at $400,000 MRR. That might mean you want to raise your prices.

Align your price with the value you create, not the cost of the value you create

You're cost ought not be an element of cost. It ought to be a component of the worth you create.

Let's say it takes you one day to fabricate a product program that saves an organization a large number of dollars. Could you just charge that organization for a day of work? No, on the grounds that the worth you made was considerably more than the cost.

So while it's vital to crease cost into the evaluating conversation to make sure you're bringing in sufficient cash, it ought not be a main consideration on the last deal (other than to set a cellar value).

<table>
<tr><td>Example</td></tr>
</table>

Monthly value

> Fuel investment funds:
> $1,000 Lubricant
> reserve funds: $100
> Savings from not expecting to employ a project worker as often as possible: $200 Incremental benefit produced: $200
> **Total value: $1,500**

- - - - - - - - - - -

> Value made by next-best other option: $1,000
> Incremental worth: $500

Monthly price

> Price of next-best option $750
> - 50% of the incremental value (assuming the value is split between you and the customer) $250
> - **Price to customer: $1,000**

In the above example, our product creates $1,500 total value a month. The next-best alternative creates $1,000 a month. So we're adding $500 of incremental value. To get our price, all we need to do is take whatever the competitor is charging ($750) and add half the incremental value. We're now charging $1,000, which is more than the competitor, but the customer is still walking away with more value ($500 vs $250).

Pricing tactics

For significant counsel in view of strong scholastic examination, I suggest Googling "Scratch Kolenda" for his rundown of estimating strategies. The subtleties of your item may not adjust impeccably with this examination, however it can fill in as a beginning stage, possibly for A/B testing your evaluating pages. Here are our #1 estimating strategies that we've utilized effectively.

1. K.I.S.S

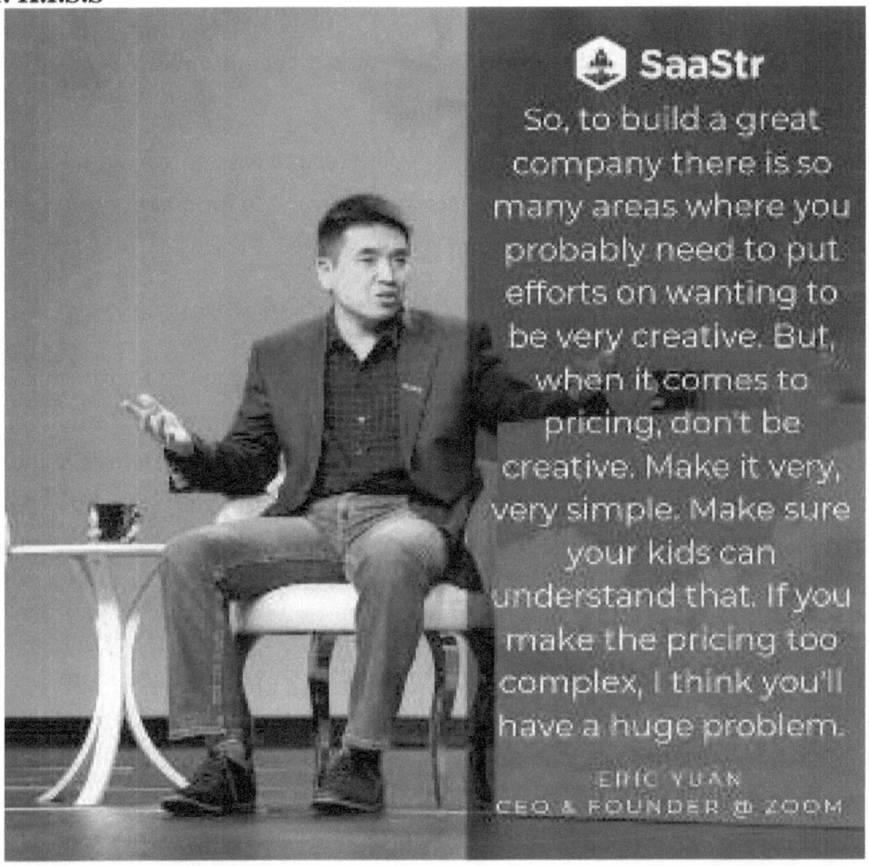

Your valuing ought to be dead-straightforward. Estimating is a very weak point for the client. They need to choose if the worth you're promising merits the cost. The best way to settle on that choice is to see the exact thing you charge. Keep it straightforward, stupid.

2. Anchor your price to something more expensive

Pretend that you've made a product item that replaces a representative whose work it is to print marks onto boxes. There are two unfathomably different estimating approaches you could utilize here:

1. Charge a cost like other SaaS items that your objective buys ($120/month)
2. Charge a large portion of the cost of the worker's compensation ($1,500/month)

This second methodology not just adjusts your cost to esteem you additionally do it so that you can undoubtedly legitimize your cost to imminent customers. You just saved them $1,500 per month!

3. **Don't underestimate the power of pricing**

One of the most central ideas in financial matters is that request increments as you bring down your costs. I've seen direct exactly the way that enormous an impact estimating changes can have on your deals execution. Your estimating page might be one of the most often visited pages on your site, so testing and improving your evaluating and bundling is definitely worth the effort.

4. **Price discriminate**

By and large, individuals ought to pay for what they use (or all the more definitively, for the worth they get). That is the reason it's essential to charge individuals diversely founded on their requirements. Generally, tech organizations charged by the quantity of clients. While this seems OK in certain unique circumstances, it's regularly skewed with the worth created.

For instance, a private venture could require three individuals getting to your product, however that doesn't mean they're willing to pay three fold the amount. But that business might be willing to pay three times as much if they started generating three times as much in revenue. In the event that your product empowers the business to significantly increase its income, it really checks out at your cost to increment close by this income hop (or some other measurement like orders delivered).

Packaging your administrations into groups is one more method for valuing segregate. The key here is to ensure clients really fall into every one of the packs. For instance, you could have 3 bundles: Small Business, Growth, and Enterprise. But it's possible that enterprise-level customers are actually buying your small plan. That implies that you've portioned your valuing inaccurately, on the grounds that you accepted bigger organizations would need the greater arrangement. It could in all likelihood be that bigger organizations esteem your enormous arrangement LESS in light of the fact that they as of now have an answer for 75% of the highlights offered.

5. **Look for quick wins**

Pricing is - and ought to be - a long and smart interaction including heaps of various stakeholders.

However, that doesn't mean there aren't fast successes that you can exploit.

For instance, In one organization I worked at, I changed the cost of each item by a couple of pennies so everything finished in 99 pennies. This made over $100,000 in steady revenue.

Another time, I changed the cost on the web and made record-breaking advertising performance.

The key in the two cases is that the estimating system was essentially consented to with various partners, leaving me allowed to tailor the specific bundling and evaluating in a coordinated manner with quick A/B testing. Eventually, this prompted an obviously better outcome than basically setting and forgetting.

Chapter summary questions

- What pricing model are you following? What levers are you pulling to change the price customers pay?

- Are you charging based on value, not on cost of service?
- Is your pricing entirely comprehensible in 7 seconds or less? Have
- you linked your pricing to an higher-value product?
- Have you constructed a system to test different pricing and packaging quickly and effectively to iterate on the best solution?
- Have you agreed the framework for your pricing and packaging?
- Do you have the buy-in, trust, and authority to run quick A/B tests to find and capture additional revenue?

BONUS SECTION!
COMMON PROBLEMS (AND THEIR SOLUTIONS)

In this last area, we will cover the most well-known go to showcase issues that we see, alongside significant, functional guidance on the best way to defeat them.

You are not winning over new prospects

In B2B item advertising, whenever qualified leads (potential open doors) are not being won by the outreach group, you ought to attempt to dig further into for what reason that is going on. To do this, you need to create a report in Salesforce or a comparative framework. Take a gander at the open doors that are "shut lost" and take a gander at the explanation codes. The reasons could be something like:

- Lost to competitor
- Timing
- Price is too high
- Not decision maker
-

Missing features

Let's say that over the most recent a half year, the outcomes were something like below:

Reason	# of lost opportunities
Lost to competitor	13
Timing	3
Price is too high	10
Not decision maker	2
Missing features	3

As you can see, the #1 explanation you are losing amazing open doors is a result of your opposition. You'll need to look further into this. Take a gander at every open door in Salesforce to distinguish which contenders appear the most:

Competitor	# of lost opportunities
A Corp	9
B Corp	1
C Corp	3

As this table shows, A Corp is one of the main reasons that you are not getting new deals. What you could find is that they offer a much lower cost than you do.

A sudden drop in website performance

One month, I encountered a sharp drop in execution of leads rolling in from a site. That month I had changed the landing page, however not without first running A/B test.

Step 1: Re-run the A/B test

The principal thing I did was re-run the A/B test. Once more, my new landing page configuration performed better with an essentially higher transformation rate.

Step 2: Isolate the problem on the website

Looking all the more intently at where the change drop was generally significant, I saw that the estimating page was the greatest giver. This all by itself was not confirmation that the evaluating page was the issue. That is on the grounds that individuals will more often than not convert on sites in light of the ENTIRE site insight, in addition to the experience of one specific page. So while the valuing page will in general produce a ton of transformations, the wide range of various pages that the guest sees add to the evaluating page conversions.

Step 3: Isolate the problem at a broader level

Looking at the information for the beyond couple of months, I recognized that estimating was the essential explanation we were not shutting possibilities, especially as for bigger prospects.

Step 4: Talk to the internal team

I addressed a business improvement rep (BDR) who let me know that he was struggling with selling our all encompassing programming in light of the fact that the possibilities previously had programming that did a lot of what we offered.

Step 5: Look at external data

I took a gander at outer information and found that about ¾ of bigger possibilities (our new objective) as of now had programming to do quite a bit of what we offered.

Conclusion

The issue was that we had changed our estimating page, in order to adjust better to our objective client which was a lot bigger than our past objective. Unexpectedly, bigger clients were very cost touchy on the grounds that they didn't esteem the all encompassing nature of our product as much since, at that size, they previously bought programming to fix numerous issues. We worked on our valuing structure and refreshed the evaluating page to improve performance.

Leads are up but pipeline is down OR leads are down but pipeline is up

A typical mental slip-up people make is partner recency with causation. This prompts issues with request age, since measurements continue on various time scales. For instance, your leads might be up for the month however your pipeline may really be down. That is on the grounds that the pipeline during the current month could be produced from last month's leads. Essentially, leads could be during this time however pipeline might be up, in light of the fact that lead age last month was strong.

It's vital to quantify results on the proper timescale. Assuming you've made a lot of changes to your greeting pages this month, then the suitable check of achievement is upgrades to your leads (structure entries like these may be characterized by "advertising drew in leads" in your organization). The effect on pipeline may not occur until the accompanying month.

Lots of leads but sales aren't going up

This is an extremely normal issue. Advertisers can have an extremely low norm for what comprises a lead, though sales reps have an exceptionally elevated requirement for what establishes a lead. So what happens is every one of those top-of-channel leads spill out in the middle.

For instance, somebody who watched an idea authority online course isn't the sort of lead a record chief needs to converse with. The top and lower part of the deals channel are simple. The genuine test is the center of the channel (i.e. MOFU). This is the place where you take the highest point of-channel leads, sustain them with instructive substance, and warm them up so that they're willing to have a discussion with a salesman, see a demo, or take part in some other high-bar offer.

A typical method for doing this is to give a progression of messages that teaches the possibility on a particular trouble spot. This could incorporate a video contextual investigation of somebody comparable who conquered the issue. It could likewise remember an email for best practices for conquering that problem area. Ultimately, you need to sell the hard deal which is the demo or consultation.

Sometimes, there is a SDR (deals advancement delegate)- otherwise called a BDR (business improvement agent)- who sits in the center among Marketing and Sales. The SDR could push the possibility to plan a demo, or the advertiser may. Progressively however, SDRs are revealing into promoting, turning into one more channel for advertisers to play in.

Another issue may be considerably further down the pipe. While you will showcase, there are destined to be a few deals developing torments. As a go to showcase pioneer, your responsibility is to ensure that deals has the capacity to close

the arrangements that advertising is conveying, which enters the universe of deals enablement.

Sales enablement is the most common way of building, conveying, and keeping up with the substance, cycles, frameworks, and apparatuses that outreach groups need close business. By and large, deals enablement as devoted job will just occur after 50-75 salespeople are employed. On the off chance that you will advertise interestingly, deals enablement will probably be possessed by showcasing (item promoting in particular).

There are many things you can do to attempt to further develop your transformation rates, yet for a first exertion, content is your smartest option. In particular, you ought to deliver inner substance to help merchants have better, more pertinent discussions. This sort of satisfied could include:

1. Battlecards

Battlecards are a short archive to help the record leaders (salesmen) land deals. The object is to set up the salespeople to answer when clients get some information about competitors.

This can be an overwhelming errand, on the grounds that the quantity of contenders could be perpetual and there could be very nuanced contrasts in highlights among the contenders. The misstep most advertisers make is that they endeavor to characterize their rivals in light of whether they offer comparable items. The main issue with this is that the serious set can turn out to be excessively huge. The subsequent issue is that possibilities won't begin naming contenders you've ever known about, or ones you never believed were qualified to be considered competitors.

The principle focus point is that clients don't characterize contenders the equivalent way
your inner item group does. All things being equal, you ought to zero in on who your "bullseye" target client is, and afterward let this definition slender down the cutthroat set. You ought to likewise take a gander at what contenders you're running into and losing arrangements to in light of your CRM data.

Once you've recognized who the key contenders are, break down them in view of your offers. For instance, assuming the fundamental advantage of your item is that it speeds up mechanical production systems, then dissect your rivals in view of that advantage. Maybe they are deficient with regards to specific key highlights that make their sequential construction systems move faster.

Typically advertisers make an expert table that subtleties every one of the contenders and the key elements they have (or don't have). I could do without this cycle since it's not client driven. In deals discussions, clients will probably name only a couple of key contenders instead of a thorough rundown, so I like to simply go through every contender individually and distinguish their lacks as far as conveying esteem. That way the salesman can rapidly take a gander at the particular contender and talk about each issue.

Try to consolidate the data into a solitary sheet.

As well as giving the lacks to every contender, ensure that your battlecard talks all the more comprehensively about where your item remains on the lookout. For instance, you could offer something like: "Dissimilar to most contenders, we offer 24 hour support," or "as a rule, our items save more in energy costs than a large portion of our competitors."

2. Sales wiki

A business wiki is only an accumulated (in a perfect world accessible) record for your outreach group about the market, the item, the objective client, and content to

send, and more.

This vault could incorporate PowerPoint slides intended to teach the outreach group on the objective client or other inside confronting materials. It could also include customer-facing materials such as handouts on specific product features, or brochures catering to specific customer groups or buying personas. For instance, you could have one freebee for CEOs that discussions about benefit and-misfortune and one more present for CTOs that discussions about IT foundation mix capabilities.

3. Crib notes

Sales reps are occupied, and are probably not going to peruse and afterward activity the more extended content that promoting produces. So part of the deliverable for deals enablement to assist with expanding close rates and deals speed is to consolidate it down into 1-2 sentences for every point. On the off chance that you can convey it logically when reps need it, that is shockingly better, yet the objective ought to be reduced down satisfied pieces that are hyper-pertinent to the rep at a particular time. Lodging notes are a simple method for conveying that value.

Large customers aren't buying

Often items go to showcase serving little organizations. Then, they "stepping stool up" to the mid-market, lastly to enterprise.

This is a proven pathway for many SaaS companies because the needs of small companies or freelancers are usually less complex and the sales cycle is shorter. But their lifetime value is usually small, so you would need to acquire a massive number of customers to build scale. It tends to be significantly simpler to scale by serving endeavor clients, when your item is adequately complex to address their issues. It's essentially useless, however, that these are not fundamentally unrelated: it's very conceivable to serve both venture clients AND little clients at the same time. Whenever I worked for a Google-upheld startup, we took special care of miniature organizations, little medium organizations, and furthermore to big business clients.

You might find it hard to offer to enormous organizations for various reasons:

- **They don't value your holistic solution**. While small companies may have appreciated the breadth of your product, you may find that large companies already have specialized products to serve most of their needs. They've already developed systems and work-arounds to get to the size they're at today. They've also already purchased products similar to yours. Your value proposition may actually narrow the further you move up market. You may need to focus more on one benefit that you deliver strongly on.

- **They don't realize customization is an option**. Large companies may dismiss your solution because they don't realize you offer thorough customizations to accommodate their workflows.

You're too expensive. Ironically, large companies may actually be more price-sensitive. This isn't because they don't have money; it's because they simply don't derive as much value from your product as smaller companies do. You may have overestimated how much more large companies are willing to pay.

You haven't enabled your account executives. Often larger companies have buying groups, and these may include multiple stakeholders who need to be sold to. As a marketer, you should develop selling tips that cater to each of those groups. For example, you may have an outline of the profit-loss impacts of your products for CEOs or general managers, and a technical product benefits sheet for engineering leads.

Event marketing is not producing qualified leads

Events can gobble up most of the promoting financial plan for B2B organizations. Contributing huge number of dollars on a solitary occasion is an unsafe speculation, yet the chance of having sharp purchasers, all gathered in a solitary spot, is excessively enticing for some organizations to miss. Anyway these high end occasions frequently don't prompt similar profit from venture as minimal expense exercises like online classes. So what's happening here?

- **Your events are not targeted enough**. Big events attract broad audiences who often don't care much for your product. You want to focus on events where the majority of attendees are your bullseye target customers—not just people who could buy our product, but the specific group that is most likely to buy it.

- **Your event attendees aren't attending with intent.** Some events attract people to evaluate solutions and buy products. But not that many. For most events, the draw to attendees is the education and sessions, not the opportunity to shop around the vendors. You want to either focus on events with the intent to buy, or change the objectives of events.

- **The majority of attendees are not customers**. Sometimes the majority of attendees at events are not actually end buyers of your product. They may actually be potential partners or collaborators. For example, the attendees may be web developers or professional service providers who cater to your end customers. You went to the event expecting new customers instead of building our your partner marketing.

The attendees are not your buyers. For B2B tech companies in particular, the end user is often not the buyer. If the majority of your attendees are end-user and not buyers, it's going to be difficult to have meaningful conversations. For example, if you sell sales automation software, you end user might be an account executive, but your buyer is the VP sales, VP marketing, or VP operations. A conference where the attendees are sales reps isn't going to generate qualified opportunities.

You've set the wrong expectations. Events have lots of auxiliary benefits beyond lead generation. Specifically, brand awareness—essentially, top of funnel impressions—and deal acceleration. Events are really good at both these things, so as a savvy marketer, you may need to change the objective of your event to match what they're good at.

PPC ads aren't producing the same results at scale

When you're little, you might see incredible outcomes with PPC advertisements once you've appropriately improved your watchwords, promotions, and greeting pages. But at a certain point, you may find that you cannot grow the advertising to get more customers cost-effectively. What's going on here?

The thing with advertising strategies like Google Ads is that they frequently work best at the lower part of-the-channel. At the end of the day, they take care of individuals who are as of now very nearly purchasing an item like yours. But the size of the bottom-of-the-funnel is always smaller than the top-of-funnel. So it's exceptionally simple to immerse the lower part of-the-pipe with catchphrases like "purchase X" or "coordination for Y."

I would say, PPC publicizing is a gauge advertising strategy. You run it ceaselessly to catch the purchase prepared possibilities, yet the genuine development will come from different strategies. For instance, you might have to a purchase rundown of 20,000 possibilities and begin hitting them with Facebook advertisements advancing your white paper. You then move those possibilities into an email succession in Outreach that sustains the prompts where they are pushed to the lower part of-the-pipe. PPC advertisements regularly hit the low-hanging fruit.

Going to market without product / market fit

This issue is generally normal assuming that you work for a beginning phase startup. What happens is that you attempt to go to advertise before you genuinely have item/market fit.

That is, you haven't situated yourself in a market where you have a demonstrated history of clients who love your item, that is adequately huge to accomplish your income objectives, and where you can express your exceptional worth over cutthroat alternatives.

Usually, this progression is surged in light of the fact that a couple of early arrangements have shut, and that drives expected item/market fit, when in actuality, those arrangements are shut due to existing associations and author selling, as opposed to genuine proof of a market looking for your solution.

Companies hurry into strategic execution and request gen without having a solid groundwork and wind up spending incapably while they sort out it on the fly.

Here are a couple of signs you probably won't have clear item/market fit:

- Every deal requires the founder / CEO / executive to be in on, regardless of deal size
- Long deal cycles for SMB / mid-market deals
- High customer churn rate
- Extremely diverse customer / user base (it's difficult to identify unifying factors)

- Low Net Promoter Score (NPS)
- Ideal Client Profile (ICP) is only loosely defined

The main fix here is to return, rethink your market choices, and observe one more specialty that you can break into with better success.

Nobody is responding to my ads or emails

Usually the issue here is that you are attempting to advance your item, organization, or brand rather than the actual deal. What I mean by the proposition is your conference, white paper, digital book, online course, demo, etc. Whenever you run direct-reaction promotions or messages, you really want to sell the deal generally with list items specifying the advantages of the offer.

Nobody is responding to my Facebook or LinkedIn ads

When you're showcasing on Facebook and LinkedIn, you're for the most part advertising to cold leads who haven't known about your organization. And that means you need to market a little differently. In the event that your promotions aren't changing over, it's likely because:

- You're trying to sell your company instead of your offer. If they've never heard of you, then you need to make sure they're getting value right away, since there's no incentive for them to click on an ad about a company they've never heard of. Content that has a low commitment for them like ebooks and whitepapers (guides) does this really well.
- You're ask is too high. Asking someone to attend an hour-long webinar is a much higher ask then getting them to download an ebook. Try lowering what you want them to do.
- You're asking for too much information. Response rates should improve if all you ask for is an email, as opposed to name, email,

company, revenue, etc.

- There's too much friction in the user experience. Response rates should also improve if you use the lead-gen forms built into the social platform, instead of sending people to your own landing page (especially for mobile traffic).

We're losing too many deals to the competition

First we should characterize the number of is too much. A decent guideline is that you ought to win somewhere in the range of 35% and 45% of the open doors you make. And of the 55% - 65% of deals that you lose, only about a third should be lost to competitors. That implies assuming you set out 100 open doors, you'll win 35 of them, you'll lose 65 of them, and of that, you'll lose around 20 to a competitor.

The rest you'll lose to different reasons (no choice, for example).

So your total rival misfortune rate ought to be something like 20% of the multitude of chances you make. At most.

If you're close/over this number, then you want to dive into the information, and execute the important strategy:

Questions to ask	Strategic response
Are you losing deals from a specific segment, company size, or industry?	Identify other segments where you're over-indexing for won deals and shift your focus to there. If you can't, you need to dig into the specific needs of the market, and reposition your product and marketing to serve it more effectively.

| Are you losing the deals for a specific reason? | Invest in product development, or pivot your product to an audience who doesn't have that specific requirement. |
| Are you being priced out of the market? | Address your messaging to better convey the value you bring that is unique over the value your |

	competitor can bring.
Are your competitors' sales processes much easier?	Streamline and simplify how you sell to make it easier for the buyer.
Is your customer experience worse?	Talk to your happy and unhappy customers. What makes one happy / unhappy? Take those happy customers and replicate that success, and tell that story during the sales cycle.

CONCLUSION

Taking an item to advertise is difficult. Richard T. James, the praised innovator of the Slinky, wound up experiencing his days in Bolivia while his phenomenally skilled spouse ran the organization as CEO.

And at this point, items are sent off consistently. Groups are collected, plans are made, crowds distinguished and advertisements are purchased. At the core of this interaction is a central conviction that anything new item you're sending off or new component you're selling will make life simpler for your objective audience.

Going to advertise is only the most common way of persuading individuals that your new way is superior to the norm.

Whether this is on the grounds that they get to invest less energy at work because of your answer that makes them 10x more effective, or it's simply a superior light, it doesn't make any difference. As you go to advertise, your main goal is to cause your crowd to have faith in what the future held, persuade them to change from doing nothing to doing something.

And to do that, you want to go through the seven stages to get to market:

1. Identify your objective audience
2. Outline the worth you bring them
3. Figure out how to tell that story
4. Build your go to showcase team
5. Define the interest and brand promoting channels that best arrive at your objective audience
6. Calculate your showcasing blend